Praying the Psalms

with

St. Padre Pio

Praying the Psalms with St. Padre Pio

Eileen Dunn Bertanzetti

Our Sunday Visitor Publishing Division
Our Sunday Visitor, Inc.
Huntington, Indiana 46750

Nihil Obstat
Rev. Michael Heintz
Censor Librorum

Imprimatur
✠ John M. D'Arcy
Bishop of Fort Wayne-South Bend
February 14, 2006

The *imprimatur* is a declaration that a work is free from doctrinal or moral error.
It is not implied that the person who has granted the *imprimatur* agrees with
the contents, opinions, or statements expressed.

The Scripture citations contained in this work are taken from the *Catholic Edition of
the New Revised Standard Version Bible* (NRSV), Copyright © 1989 and 1993 by the
Division of Christian Education of the National Council of the Churches of Christ
in the United States of America. Used by permission. All rights reserved.

St. Padre Pio's quotes are taken from *Padre Pio of Pietrelcina's Letters, Volumes I, II,*
and *III*, Copyrights © 1985, 1987, 1994, respectively, by San Giovanni Rotondo.
Used with permission.

Every reasonable effort has been made to determine copyright holders of excerpted
materials and to secure permissions as needed. If any copyrighted materials have been
inadvertently used in this work without proper credit being given in one form or
another, please notify Our Sunday Visitor in writing so that future printings of this
work may be corrected accordingly.

Our Sunday Visitor Publishing Division
Our Sunday Visitor, Inc.
200 Noll Plaza
Huntington, IN 46750

ISBN-13: 978-1-59276-197-5
ISBN-10: 1-59276-197-6 (Inventory No. T248)
LCCN: 2006921705

Cover design and illustration by Rebecca J. Heaston
Interior design by Sherri L. Hoffman

Printed in the United States of America

Acknowledgments

✝

I would like to acknowledge the following: Our Sunday Visitor's acquisitions editor Jackie Lindsey and project editor Darrin Malone; my patient husband Greg; my parents Norm and Marie Dunn; my children, children-in-law, and grandchildren; all my friends, including Fr. Daniel J. O'Neill, Msgr. Timothy P. Stein, and the staff of The Institute of Children's Literature; Fr. Alessio Parente, O.F.M. Cap., of San Giovanni Rotondo, Italy, for giving me permission to quote St. Padre Pio's letters; our Blessed Virgin Mother; St. Padre Pio; my holy guardian angel; and, of course, God the Father, Son, and Holy Spirit.

Contents

✠

Introduction

+╬+

Throughout the eighty-one years of his life, Padre Pio — proclaimed "St. Pio of Pietrelcina" by Pope John Paul II on June 16, 2002 — experienced within himself every human emotion, including fear, sorrow, remorse, and guilt. Where did St. Padre Pio turn for help and guidance, strength and comfort? One source on which he relied was the Bible, and in particular the Psalms. For example, on October 17, 1915, in a state of spiritual dryness, when he felt as if God had abandoned him, as if God were "hiding" from him, Padre Pio found reassurance by recalling two of the Psalms in which the Psalmist expresses the same anguish. In his letter that day, Pio said to God, "My spirit faints.... My soul languishes for your salvation" (Psalm 77:3, 119:81). Immediately, in the same letter, St. Pio said to God, "You can see what suffering this is for the soul that seeks You, oh my Lord. I would bear this pain in peace for love of You, if only I knew that even in this state I am not forsaken by You, oh Source of eternal happiness!"[1] Toward the end of Psalm 119, Pio found the reassurance and comfort he needed: *Your word is a lamp to my feet and a light to my path.... You are my hiding place and my shield.... Your faithfulness endures to all generations.*[2]

Yes, just as David and the other Psalmists, throughout the 150 Psalms, experienced every basic human emotion and misery that you have felt, so, too, did St. Padre Pio. Even now, from heaven, Pio can identify and empathize with you as you carry your daily cross, and he can rejoice with you in your inevitable joy.

Who Is This Saint?

For fifty years, as a monastic priest in San Giovanni Rotondo, Italy, St. Pio bore the stigmata, the five wounds of Christ Crucified. For fifty years, those wounds bled every day and caused Pio's hands to swell, his side to throb, and his feet to ache.

Stigmata

Through spiritual as well as bodily fevers, Padre Pio continued to suffer. During every moment of every trial, he trusted in Jesus and found joy in Him.

In March 1919, Pio wrote to a friend who had asked how Pio had received the stigmata, "Since September 20 of last year, after the appearances of a heavenly personage, [Christ Crucified], I found my hands and feet pierced and an open wound close to the heart. I don't want you to begin to hold me, a wretch, in high regard as a result of this revelation. Admire the marvels of the Lord and nothing else."[3]

Take Heart

Echoing Psalm 40:1-2, St. Padre Pio said, "Live tranquilly and don't be bewildered in the dark night through which your spirit is passing. Be patient and resigned while awaiting the return of your divine Sun who will soon come to brighten the forest of your spirit."[4]

Why did Pio have such undying confidence in Christ? Through his own experiences with pain, poverty, frail health, and other trials, Pio learned to "take heart; it is Jesus who permits your soul to be in a state of aridity, in darkness. . . . The Lord wants to lead you amidst the thorns because He wants you to be similar to Him."[5]

Some of His Other Gifts

For fifty years, Padre Pio bore the gift of the stigmata. Wasn't that enough for one person to endure? Apparently not. In order to help people, God also blessed Pio with the gift of bilocation — the ability to be in two places at one time.

Pio had the gift of perfume. Many times when he wanted people to know he was praying for them and that God would meet their needs, the people would smell violets, lilies, or roses. In Confession, Padre Pio had the ability to read a person's soul. If the person concealed sins from him, Pio would reveal them to that person.

God also granted Pio the gift of conversion. Countless people returned to Jesus and to the Church through Padre Pio's intercession.

By Christ's power, St. Pio healed the sick in body, mind, and soul. Padre Pio also prophesied. During World War Two, he told the people of San Giovanni Rotondo that no bombs would hit that city. With a foreign-occupied air base only fifteen miles away, the people refused to believe their Padre. But when the war ended and no bombs had struck their town, they believed.

Though Padre Pio received more than his share of spiritual gifts, he never sought them. He never felt worthy of them. He never put the gifts before the Giver. About supernatural gifts, Pio wrote, "You must by no means desire such extraordinary things, knowing that it is not these things that render the soul more perfect, but rather, holy Christian virtue."[6]

Pilgrims from Around the World

St. Pio's spiritual gifts attracted pilgrims from all over the world. People traveled to the rocky, barren land on which San Giovanni perched. They wanted to see, touch, hear, and even smell this now-famous priest. Because Pio hated to be the center of attention, his popularity caused him inner pain. But despite all his afflictions of body and soul, he continued to trust Christ and to find great joy in God. And Padre Pio continued to take comfort in the Psalms: "From long experience," Pio said, "I know there is absolutely no way Jesus will either remove or alleviate all those gifts He has given me up to now. So I will stretch myself out on this cross, also in a placid manner, and with a serene soul."[7]

Heavenly Homeland

By 1968, the year of St. Pio's death, millions of people revered him. Thousands of the faithful attended his daily Masses. Pio *lived* the Mass and often fell into ecstasy, in love with God present in the Eucharist.

No matter what troubles assailed him, Pio refused to let his "heart be troubled."[8] Like the Psalmist, Pio trusted God. "Pay no attention to the path of trial," Pio wrote. "Keep your eyes constantly fixed on He who guides you to the heavenly homeland. Why should the soul be despondent? . . . Believe me, Jesus is with you, so what do you fear?"[9]

No matter what miseries you face, remember Psalm 107 in which God assures you of his faithfulness. He promises to bring you out of your "distress" and to "hush" the "waves of the sea" of your troubles. And remember, too, what St. Padre Pio said, "Call to mind the words the divine Master said to the apostles, and which He says to you today, 'Do not let your hearts be troubled.'[10]"[11]

Milestones in St. Pio's Life

✠

1887, May 25 — born in Pietrelcina, Italy

1903, January — enters Capuchin Novitiate in Morcone

1910, August — ordained in Cathedral of Benevento

1918, September — receives stigmata

1947, May — inaugurates Home for the Relief of Suffering

1968, September 22 — celebrates last Mass

1968, September 23 — dies

1997, December 18 — proclaimed "Venerable"

1999, Spring — beatification

2002, June 16 — canonization — proclaimed "St. Pio of Pietrelcina"

I
He Watches Over You

✠

From Psalm 1: "Happy are those who do not follow the advice of the wicked, or take the path that sinners tread, . . . but their delight is in the law of the LORD, . . . [And] the LORD watches over the way of the righteous . . ."[1]

But how can I lead a "righteous" life when our culture promotes evil?

ST. PIO'S WORDS

"The divine Lover reserves great glory in heaven for those souls who continue steadfastly to do His will at all times."[2]

"What else do you desire, then, if not that God's plan may be fulfilled in you? Take courage, therefore, and go forward on the path of divine Love, with the firm conviction that the more fully your own will becomes united and conformed to God's will, the more you will advance toward perfection. Always keep before your eyes the fact that here on earth we are on a battlefield and that in paradise we'll receive the crown of victory. . . .[3]

"Praise be to God in the highest heavens! He is my strength; He is the salvation of my soul; He is my portion forever. In Him I hope, in Him I trust, and I will fear no evil."[4]

PRAYER

In my trials, please help me believe You are always watching over me.

2
Your Refuge

✣

From Psalm 2: "Happy are all who take refuge in him."[1]

But when my enemies attack and life threatens to overwhelm me, will I remember to "take refuge" in God?

ST. PIO'S WORDS

"You must by no means fear that the Lord will leave you at your enemy's mercy. God is faithful, and He never allows you to be tempted beyond your strength.[2] God gives your enemies just as much power to torment you as serves His own fatherly plan for the sanctification of your soul and for the greater glory of His divine Majesty. Hence, you must be strong and cheerful in spirit, for the Lord is in the depths of your heart: He will fight along with you and for you. Who, then, will win the battle? Who is stronger than He? Who will hold out against the King of the heavens? . . . What is hell itself in front of the Lord? Hold resolutely to the comforting thought that God is with you all the time and will never abandon you to your enemy's attacks."[3]

PRAYER

Always remind me that nothing *is more powerful than You and Your love.*

3
Your Shield

✠

From Psalm 3: "O LORD, how many are my foes! . . . But you, O LORD, are a shield around me, my glory, and the one who lifts up my head."[1]

When "foes" surround me, it's hard to believe Jesus is even with *me.*

ST. PIO'S WORDS

"What more can I say? Jesus, whom you call and believe you have lost, is totally yours. [Because] He is so tightly united to you, more than ever you must believe that you possess Him. What do you fear then? Listen to God who says to Abraham, and to you also: 'Do not be afraid.'[2] What do you seek on earth if not God? Well then, I tell you in the name of God Himself, that you possess Him. Be firm in your resolutions, stay in the boat in which Jesus has placed you, and let the storms come. . . . You will not perish. To you He appears to be sleeping, but at the opportune time, He will awaken to restore your calm. . . . Why are you afraid? No, do not fear; you are walking on the sea amid the wind and waves, but you are surely with Jesus. What is there to fear?"[3]

PRAYER

Lord, when "storms" threaten, help me to find my peace in You. Amen.

4
When You Are Disturbed or Angry

✠

From Psalm 4: "When you are [angry], do not sin; ponder it . . . and be silent."[1]

What if anger tries to force me to do unholy acts or to say harsh words?

ST. PIO'S WORDS

"Especially do I ask divine love for you. This is everything for you. It is the honey which must sweeten all your weaknesses, feelings, and actions. . . . Under obedience to God and in His realm [within you], He does not allow serious sins to dwell. . . .

"It is true that God allows them to arrive at [your mind and senses] so that, in the combat, the virtues may be practiced and strengthened. He even allows the master spies — venial sins and imperfections — to circulate freely in His kingdom, but this is merely to show you that, without Him, you would be a prey for your enemies. . . . Humble yourself deeply and confess that if God were not your breastplate and shield, you would at once be pierced by every kind of sin."[2]

PRAYER

Lord, when anger seethes inside me, demanding revenge on those who offend me, help me let go of the anger and turn away from sin. Amen.

5
The Power of His Name

✠

From Psalm 5: "Spread your protection over them, [Lord], so that those who love your name may exult in you."[1]

But why would I want to actually love the Lord's name?

ST. PIO'S WORDS

"The eternal Father decreed that all creatures should be subject to Him: 'so that at the name of Jesus every knee should bend, in heaven and on earth and under the earth.'[2] This is true. Jesus is adored in heaven.

"This most holy name is venerated on earth, and all the graces you ask in Jesus' name are granted by the eternal Father [John 14:13].... This divine name is venerated even in hell!... This name is terror to the demons, who are broken and vanquished by it: '[By using] my name they will cast out demons.'[3]

"Through Jesus' obedience, the heavenly Father willed that all creatures should confess and believe in this most holy name: '... every tongue should confess that Jesus Christ is Lord, to the glory of God the Father.'[4]"[5]

PRAYER

Jesus, please help me to always love and respect your name in thought, word, and action. Amen.

6
God Hears You Weep

From Psalm 6: "I am weary with my moaning; every night I flood my bed with tears. . . . [But] the LORD has heard the sound of my weeping. . . . All my enemies shall be ashamed and struck with terror."[1]

But why does God allow bad things to happen to me in the first *place? Is He punishing me for my sins and failings?*

ST. PIO'S WORDS

"Give free reign to your tears, by all means, because this is the work of the Lord. . . . Your infirmities, temptations . . . aridity, and desolation all come from His infallible love. . . . He wants you to be similar to His beloved Son in the anxiety of the desert, of the Garden, and on the cross. And when the evil one wants to persuade you that you are a victim of his assaults, or of divine abandonment, don't believe him, because he is suggesting something that is not true; he wants to trick you. It is not true that you . . . disgust the Lord, and therefore, it is not true that the Lord has not forgiven you your faults or your deviations in the past. Divine grace is with you, and you are very dear to the Lord."[2]

PRAYER

Dear Jesus, help me to accept my sufferings, as You did Yours. Amen.

7

When the Lion Pursues

✠

From Psalm 7: "O LORD my God, . . . save me from all my pursuers, and deliver me, or like a lion they will tear me apart; they will drag me away, with no one to rescue [me]."[1]

But what if the "lion" attacks before I can ask God to help me?

ST. PIO'S WORDS

"'Discipline yourselves, and keep alert. Like a roaring lion your adversary the devil prowls around, looking for someone to devour. Resist him, steadfast in your faith.'[2]"[3]

"Let this unhappy enemy create an uproar; let him even threaten to swallow you up; it doesn't matter, for he can achieve nothing against your soul, which Jesus has now clasped to Himself and sustains in a mysterious manner by His ever-present grace."[4]

". . . Don't fear the gloomy wrath of the evil one. . . . It is a good sign when he . . . roars around your will. This shows he is not within you."[5]

"May Jesus bless you and save you from the roaring lion!"[6]

PRAYER

Oh Jesus, please enable me to always be "disciplined and alert" so that I always recognize evil and resist it by putting my faith in You. Amen.

8

Unworthy?

✠

From Psalm 8: "When I look at your heavens . . . what are human beings that you are mindful of them, mortals that you care for them? Yet you have made them a little lower than God."[1]

I cry out to God, "Lord, I'm a sinner, unworthy to even consider myself a little lower *than You. Sometimes my weaknesses horrify me."*

ST. PIO'S WORDS

"Your cries and shouts? These are only too natural in one who is frightened, and God who causes them does not reproach you for them, just as He did not rebuke His only begotten Son on the cross, where He knew He had been placed by the Father's will, though He cried out that He was forsaken.

"Where, then, is your present unworthiness and wickedness of heart? You may be horrified, certainly, by the sight of what you might have been and still could be, but rejoice and thank the divine Mercy that you are not what you might have been. Be consoled and have no fear."[2]

"May Jesus always render you more worthy of His divine embraces."[3]

PRAYER

Lord, in Your mercy, and by Your grace, make me always worthy. Amen.

9
Your Stronghold

✠

From Psalm 9: "The LORD is a stronghold for the oppressed, a stronghold in times of trouble."[1]

But how can I live a godly life in this troubled and anti-God world?

ST. PIO'S WORDS

"Do not let the persecutions from the world and all those who live without the Spirit of Jesus Christ deter you from following the road trodden by the saints. Continue to run up the steep slope of the mountain of holiness and don't let the rough path dismay you. Continue to walk close to Jesus, and if following Him means protection against every mishap, you will most certainly win in all things. . . .

"Before breathing your last on the cross, you still have to agonize in the Garden with Jesus Christ. Don't be frightened, however. . . . The Lord will continue to pour out upon you not only the oil of His gladdening mercy, but the oil of His virtue which will strengthen you and make you successful in the combat. . . . Carry on tranquilly, for the divine Mercy will not be lacking . . . if you show docility beneath the Lord's divine action."[2]

PRAYER

Lord, replace my fears with total trust in Your mercy and grace. Amen.

10
When God Hides

✠

From Psalm 10: "Why, O LORD, do you stand far off? Why do you hide yourself in times of trouble?"[1]

Why does God seem to hide whenever troubles afflict me?

ST. PIO'S WORDS

"Do not fear. . . . He who has helped you up to now will continue His work of salvation. You will be saved; the enemy will fume with rage. Be sure that the hand which has sustained you up to now — making you enumerate countless victories — that same hand will continue to sustain you until the point when your soul will hear itself invited by the heavenly Bridegroom: 'Come, my bride. Take the crown I have prepared for you from eternity.' Have boundless trust in the Lord because your reward is not far away. The prophet's words will not delay in being verified: 'Then your light shall rise in the darkness.'[2]"[3]

"Therefore, be consoled in the Lord because your soul has chosen God as its portion. Jesus is with you. He has helped you up to now. He cannot and does not want to abandon you; He will perfect His work."[4]

PRAYER

Lord, I surrender myself — forever — into Your ever-faithful arms. Amen.

11

The Future

✠

From Psalm 11: "The LORD tests the righteous and the wicked, and his soul hates the lover of violence."[1]

I, too, hate violence, but in this violent world filled with hatred for life, peace, and God, I sometimes fear I will succumb to violent behavior.

ST. PIO'S WORDS

"It is about time you rid yourself, once and for all, of so many foolish and unfounded fears which pass through your mind, weigh upon your heart, and keep it bound with harsh chains. Do you entertain doubts about the future? But have I not assured you that the Lord is always with you? Is not the future the same as the present in the sight of the Lord? What then do you doubt? ... Yes, you are afraid of acting badly and offending God. But rest assured, and be quite at peace, for the ever-present grace of Jesus will take good care to save you from being unfaithful.

"Calm your immoderate fear, for I assure you in Jesus' name that as long as you live, you will always do His will. Grace will not be lacking."[2]

PRAYER

Lord, cause me to always remember: "It is no longer I who live, but it is Christ who lives in me,"[3] and in my weakness, Lord, You are strong.[4] Amen.

12
Make Us Worthy, Father

✠

From Psalm 12:1 "Help, O LORD, for there is no longer anyone who is godly; the faithful have disappeared."[1]

It does seem that the world is filled with — and controlled by — ungodly people, and I wonder how I can resist their influence and live a godly life.

ST. PIO'S WORDS

"How exceedingly the Son loves us, and at the same time what excessive humility is His in asking the Father to allow Him to remain with us [in the Eucharist] until the end of the world! Again, what exceeding love has the Father for us, when He has seen Jesus subjected to such dreadful treatment and still permits this beloved Son of His to remain among us [in the Eucharist], to be the target of fresh insults every day! . . . How can Your most-merciful Heart, Father, bear to see Your only begotten Son so neglected . . . and sacrilegiously received . . . by so many unworthy Christians?

". . . Father, give us today our daily bread. Give us Jesus always during our brief stay in this land of exile. Give Him to us and grant that we may be increasingly worthy to welcome Him into our hearts."[2]

PRAYER

Father, always make me worthy to receive Jesus in the Eucharist.

13
You're Never Alone

✠

From Psalm 13: "How long, O LORD? Will you forget me forever? . . . How long must I bear pain in my soul, and have sorrow
in my heart?"[1]

When suffering steals into my life, I feel as if God has forgotten me.

ST. PIO'S WORDS

"Do not say that you are all alone in climbing Calvary and that
you are all alone as you struggle and weep, for Jesus is with you
and will never abandon you. . . . I beg you to calm your anxiety and
apprehension on this score. Remain at peace, continue to go forward, and don't let your holy course be stopped. I assure you, in
our most-tender Lord, that you are already halfway to the summit
of Calvary. It is true that this is the darkest hour of the night for
you, but may the thought of a bright dawn and a more brilliant
noontime sustain you, cheer you, and induce you to keep moving
forward. Do not doubt that the One who has sustained you so far
will continue with ever greater patience and divine kindness to
support you on the remainder of your difficult and trying journey."[2]

PRAYER

*Forgive me, Lord, for thinking you've forgotten me. Even in my dark-
est hours, help me to place my trust in You. Thank You. Amen.*

14
The Joy of Your Nothingness

✠

From Psalm 14: "Fools say in their hearts, 'There is no God.'"[1]

When my enemies threaten to overcome me, sometimes I, too, doubt God.

ST. PIO'S WORDS

"I understand that your enemies are very strong, but when you fight along with Jesus, how can you have any doubt about winning the battle? Isn't our dear God stronger than all the others? . . . Has He not promised He will not allow you to be tempted beyond your strength?[2] Is He unfaithful to His promises? Do you want to know who believes this? It is the fool, the madman: The fool says in his heart, 'There is no God.'[3]

"The person who sins through disbelief and lack of trust is a madman. You, now more than ever, have not just *one* proof of divine promises, but an infinite number of proofs . . . . These are as numerous as the victories your soul has won over its enemies. Without divine grace, could you have been victorious in all the crises and spiritual battles you have faced? Open your soul to divine hope, and trust in divine Mercy. . . . God is always ready to raise you up if . . . you acknowledge your nothingness before Him."[4]

PRAYER

Lord, keep me humble; remind me that I am nothing without You. Amen.

15
Master of Your Heart

✠

From Psalm 15: "O LORD, who may abide in your tent? . . . Those who walk blamelessly, and do what is right, and speak the truth."[1]

I do want to "walk blamelessly," but I'm not perfect; sometimes I fail. How will I ever reach heaven, God's "tent"?

ST. PIO'S WORDS

"You have profound determination to serve God, and this indicates that you will be faithful to devout practices and to the constant effort to acquire virtue. But I warn you of one thing of which you're not aware: When you fail in some way due to weakness, you should not be surprised, but while detesting, on the one hand, the offence to God, on the other, you must conceive a joyful humility at the sight and knowledge of your miseries."[2]

"Therefore, do not be upset, whatever your state. Let yourself be guided lovingly by divine Providence, whether He wants you to walk on land, in the desert, or through the waters of sensitive and spiritual consolations."[3]

"Live humbly, docile and in love with our unique heavenly Spouse, and may He alone be the Master of your heart."[4]

PRAYER

Lord, I give myself to You. Forever be Master of my heart. Amen.

16

Divine Goodness

✠

From Psalm 16: "Protect me, O God, for in you I take refuge. I say to the LORD, 'You are my Lord; I have no good apart from you.'"[1]

Apart from God, I have no merits, love, or goodness, but what if I succumb to the world's evil and stop loving and living for divine goodness?

ST. PIO'S WORDS

"How much you will be indebted to divine goodness, which makes you so ardently desire to live and die in His love. You yearn for this; you are determined; you hope and trust that this good Savior, who gives you the will, will also give you the grace to carry it out. . . . By His holy love, the supreme Goodness will keep the nest of your heart safe from the assaults of the world. He will keep you from being submerged."[2]

"Rest your heart in God alone, and no longer take it away from Him. He is your peace, consolation, [goodness], and your glory. Make every effort to unite yourself more tightly to this most-sweet Savior, so that you can produce good fruit for eternal life. . . . This sovereign Being is the Root of the tree of which we are the branches, and our good works the fruit."[3]

PRAYER

Lord, please keep me always grafted to You and bearing good fruit.

17
Are You Listening, God?

✠

From Psalm 17: "Hear a just cause, O LORD; attend to my cry."[1]

I cry out to Jesus, but He doesn't seem to answer. Has He left me?

ST. PIO'S WORDS

"You seek your God; you sigh for Him, call Him, but cannot see any trace of Him. God seems to hide Himself; to abandon you."[2]

"Jesus has not abandoned you, nor will He. On the contrary, in that painful state in which your soul is immersed, Jesus is closer to you, clasped tightly to your heart. In fact, this desire of yours to seek Him comes from Jesus; your sighs come from Jesus; your complaints come from Jesus; everything within you comes from Jesus. He permits the trial for His glory and for your good. Suffice it for you to know this.

"In moments of spiritual oppression, place yourself in the presence of God and pronounce your *Fiat* — 'Thy will be done!' I know that sometimes you will not have strength to do this, but do not fear. . . . It is sufficient that you know that Jesus is pleased with you and that you are on the true path."[3]

PRAYER

Lord, when physical, emotional, or spiritual oppressions trouble me, help me to trust in Your presence and to thank You, even for my trials. Amen.

18
Your Will, Not Your Feelings

✠

From Psalm 18: "I love you, O LORD, my strength."[1]

But most of the time, I don't feel any love for God, even though, every day, I offer my life to Him and tell Him how much I love and need Him.

ST. PIO'S WORDS

"Let it be sufficient for you to be united to God by your will. You are afraid you are not united to Him, even by your will, and this causes you interior torment. Cast off your doubts! Your will is united with God's will. A person who does not love God does not pay any attention to Him, does not fear *not* loving Him, and never thinks of God with the sincere desire to love Him.... Console yourself that as long as you fear you do not love God, and as long as you fear offending Him, you already love Him and no longer offend Him. If everyone felt the fear you feel, no one would offend God."[2]

"Console yourself and be quite sure that God is not found where there is no desire to love Him. If your soul longs for nothing else than to love God — which is your case — don't worry, and be quite sure that your soul possesses everything, that it possesses God Himself."[3]

PRAYER

Lord, I give You my life, love, and will. Unite me always to You. Amen.

19
When Love and Fear Kiss

✠

From Psalm 19: "The fear of the LORD is pure, enduring forever."[1]

But I thought that loving *God was supposed to be my priority, not* fearing *Him.*

ST. PIO'S WORDS

"You must continually implore two things from our most-tender Lord: that He increase within you love and fear, for this will make you fly in the ways of the Lord. It will make you careful where you set foot, make you see the things of the world for what they are, and lead you to beware of all negligence. Then, when love and fear kiss, it will no longer be in your power to give your affections to the things of this world. You will no longer experience strife or envy. Your only desire on this earth will be to delight the loved One. . . . You shall advance cautiously, but with holy freedom. You shall feel that the Lord, who has chained you to Him by love, is leading you to beware of sin as of a poisonous viper. And while you take the greatest care to never commit deliberate sin, you will have a greater fear of mortal sin than of fire."[2]

PRAYER

Lord, increase in me holy love and fear, so that I'll always delight You.

20

Secret of the Cross

✠

From Psalm 20: "The LORD [will] answer you in the day of trouble!"[1]

But I don't always like *His answers, especially when my troubles linger.*

ST. PIO'S WORDS

"Trust in God and hope that, in His fatherly goodness, He will let His light come [into the darkness of your troubles]. Lift up your mind, full of faith, to your heavenly home, and may all your yearnings and aspirations be directed there. Admire the heavenly regions which can be reached by no other road than that of suffering. Heaven is your true home. What does it matter if you reach it by treading no other paths than the rough ones of tribulation and sacrifice?

"... In order to reach your final goal, you must follow your divine Leader, who usually leads chosen souls by the path He Himself trod ... by the path of self-denial and suffering: 'If any want to become my followers, let them deny themselves and take up their cross and follow me.'[2] Consider yourself fortunate to see yourself treated in this way by Jesus. Foolish are those who fail to fathom the secret of the cross."[3]

PRAYER

Lord, help me to always follow You and to embrace my cross. Amen.

21
More Powerful Than Hell

✠

From Psalm 21: "Be exalted, O LORD, in your strength! We will sing and praise your power."[1]

When everyday problems weigh me down, where is God's strength? How can I praise His power when everything looks so hopeless?

ST. PIO'S WORDS

"You must have boundless faith in the divine goodness, for the victory is absolutely certain. How could you think otherwise? Isn't our God more concerned about our salvation than we are ourselves? Isn't He stronger than hell itself? Who can ever resist and overcome the King of the heavens? What are the world, the devil, the flesh, and all your enemies before the Lord?"[2]

"Humble yourself a great deal and confess that if God were not your armor and shield, you would immediately be pierced with all kinds of sin."[3]

"Therefore, do not fear. Jesus is more powerful than all hell, and at the invocation of His holy name, all knees in heaven, earth, and hell will bend, to the consolation of the good and the terror of the wicked."[4]

PRAYER

Praise You, Lord, for Your power and love which daily rescue me. Amen.

22
Abandoned

✠

From Psalm 22: "My God, my God, why have you forsaken me?"[1]

This world is filled with darkness and despair, and all I hear is bad news. Evil seems to surround me, and I conclude that God has finally deserted me.

ST. PIO'S WORDS

"You see yourself to be abandoned, but I assure you that Jesus is holding you more tightly than ever to his divine Heart. Even our Lord on the cross complained of the Father's abandonment.[2] But did the Father ever, and *could* He ever really have abandoned His Son? You're experiencing the supreme trials of the spirit. Jesus wants them, so exclaim, '*Fiat*! God's will be done!' Pronounce this *fiat* with resignation whenever you are in a state of trial, and do not fear."[3]

"How could Jesus possibly permit the destruction of the whole, long, loving, indescribable work of His grace in you? This is impossible, for He always remains the God of goodness, omnipotence, and love."[4]

"I feel in my soul a holy joy by reason of God's great love for you. The storm which rages around you is a sure sign of this love."[5]

PRAYER

Lord, thanks for never deserting me. Hold me and never let go. Amen.

23

True Paths

✠

From Psalm 23: "He leads me in right paths for his name's sake."[1]

But why do those "right paths" have to be so rough, winding, and uphill?

ST. PIO'S WORDS

"Jesus chose the cross as His standard, so He wants all His followers to tread the path to Calvary, carrying the cross. . . . Only this way do you reach salvation."[2]

"Remember that the children of Israel were in the desert for forty years before reaching the promised land. . . . It was not right for them to question the reason why God led them through rough and winding paths. All those who complained did not set foot in the promised land, but perished. . . . Courage, I beg you! Pay no attention to the path of trial, but keep your eyes constantly fixed on Him who guides you to the heavenly homeland."[3]

"Our sweet Savior will grant you the enlightenment to follow the true path. . . . You must only have courage. [Your desire] to serve God is a sure sign that you will tightly embrace this service. . . . Serve God with a joyful spirit because God is the God of joy."[4]

PRAYER

Lord, lead me wherever You will, and fill me always with Your joy. Amen.

24
The Face of God

+

From Psalm 24: "Those who seek him, who seek the face of the God of Jacob.... They will receive blessings from the LORD."[1]

I do seek God and His face, and I know I'll see Him "face to face" in heaven, but all I can do here is imagine *His face. Help me do that, please.*

ST. PIO'S WORDS

"Oh, [just imagine] how beautiful is Jesus' face, how sweet His eyes, and what a good thing it is to stay close to Him."[2]

"Try to see a certain lovable majesty in His presence, a certain pleasant authority in His manner of speaking, a certain pleasant dignity in His walking . . . a certain sweet serenity of face. Imagine the extremely composed and sweet expression with which He drew the crowds, making them leave cities and castles, leading them to the mountains, the forests, to solitude, and to the deserted beaches of the sea, totally forgetting food, drink, and their domestic duties. . . . Do your utmost to be, as far as possible, similar to Him on this earth, in order to be more perfect and more similar to Him for the whole of eternity in the heavenly Jerusalem."[3]

PRAYER

Make me more like You so that I will someday see Your face in heaven. Amen.

25
What If?

✠

From Psalm 25: "For your name's sake, O LORD, pardon my guilt, for it is great."[1]

But what if God does not forgive my sins? Will my soul go to hell?

ST. PIO'S WORDS

"What are you afraid of with regard to your soul? Don't you know that Jesus is with you and is doing everything within you? Calm yourself and do not heed those vain and useless fears. Fill up your heart with ardent love for God. Humble yourself beneath God's powerful hand and always accept cheerfully and humbly the trials He sends you, so that at the time of His visitation He may raise you up by His grace. Cast all your cares upon Him, for He is more concerned about you than a mother is for her little child.

"Keep your eyes fixed on Jesus who climbs the hill of Calvary loaded with His cross, . . . see Him followed by an immense throng of holy souls carrying their own crosses. . . . Look to the end of the journey and don't separate yourself from them . . . refuse to follow any other way."[2]

PRAYER

Lord, keep my eyes fixed on You, as I follow You by following Your saints, including Your most holy Virgin Mother, Queen of the saints. Amen.

26
How to Reach Heaven, God's House

‡

From Psalm 26: "O LORD, I love the house in which you dwell, and the place where your glory abides."[1]

Thoughts of heaven do fill me with love and longing, but how can I ever reach God's "house" if I'm always struggling up my own "Mount Calvary"?

ST. PIO'S WORDS

"Oh how happy you must consider yourself to be, if you make the effort to live there [on Mount Calvary], faithfully and lovingly, in order to adore Jesus Crucified in this life. In that way, you will be certain of adoring Jesus Glorified in the next life.

". . . The inhabitants of that hill [Mount Calvary] must be stripped of all worldly affections, just as their King was stripped of the clothes He wore. . . . It was right that our divine Master should be stripped, to show you that nothing profane must be brought to this hill, and to show that Calvary, that mystical stairway to paradise, is not for those who do otherwise."[2]

"May Jesus and the most holy Virgin make you worthy of eternal glory."[3]

PRAYER

Please help me to carry my cross up that "stairway" to You in heaven. Amen.

27
Possess Me, Lord

✠

From Psalm 27: "The LORD is the stronghold of my life; of whom shall I be afraid?"[1]

Sometimes I fear that the powers of evil and of the flesh will overcome me, will even overpower God's grace within me.

ST. PIO'S WORDS

"Place your unlimited trust in the divine goodness. The more violent the enemy becomes, the more you should abandon yourself trustfully on the breast of our most-tender heavenly Spouse, who will never allow you to be overcome. . . . Even St. Paul was restless and asked the Lord to free him from his trials. Paul, too, was afraid that he would yield, but he received the assurance that grace would always be sufficient for him.[2] Our enemy wants to persuade you that the opposite is true, but despise him in the name of Jesus and laugh heartily at him. This is the best way to make him retreat."[3]

"God is with you, and hell, the world, and the flesh will one day relinquish their weapons and admit they are powerless against the soul that possesses and is possessed by God."[4]

PRAYER

Jesus, possess me so that evil can never be a part of my life. Amen.

28

Carry Me, Lord

✠

From Psalm 28: "O save your people, and bless your heritage; be their shepherd, and carry them forever."[1]

But where is this Shepherd? I don't feel His presence. I need Him.

ST. PIO'S WORDS

"Do not fear, because God is both inside and outside of you. By pouring Himself into your interior, He will surround your 'walls.' Like an open shell in the ocean, you will drink your fill, and exuberantly you will be carried along by His power."[2]

" . . . Admire the goodness of our Lord, who has come so promptly to your aid to remove you from the path you were treading so heedlessly and which ended in a precipice. . . . Jesus' grace was so powerful that it was not confined to enlightening you and warning you of the danger. . . . He drew you to Himself by the power of love without encroaching in the slightest on your own free will. You felt this loving power and could only yield to it. . . . He is always close to you; He rules, protects, and sustains you, so that your will may not be overcome by your enemies."[3]

PRAYER

Lord, rule, protect, and sustain me; be my Shepherd forever. Amen.

29

Stretched Out on the Cross

✠

From Psalm 29: "May the LORD give strength to his people! May the LORD bless his people with peace!"[1]

How can I find peace when I'm burdened with worries that weaken me?

ST. PIO'S WORDS

"May Jesus continue to be the supreme King of your heart. I say continue, because He already is such, and this must comfort you in the terrible crisis through which you are passing. Be resigned and, if possible, at peace. . . . You are suffering, but be resigned so that you can say with the prophet, 'Surely it was for my welfare that I had great bitterness; but you have held back my life from the pit of destruction.'[2]

"Your suffering is willed by Him who wants to render you similar to His only begotten Son. You are suffering, yes, but don't be afraid, because He who keeps you stretched out on the cross loves you and is giving you the strength to bear the unbearable."[3]

"Live happily and at peace, and be clothed in Jesus Christ."[4]

PRAYER

If I have to suffer to be more like You, Jesus, I accept whatever suffering You send. I trust You to give me the strength and peace to bear it. Amen.

30

Just Wait

✠

From Psalm 30: "Weeping may linger for the night, but joy comes with the morning."[1]

When darkness presses down on me, I can't find God — let alone find His joy.

ST. PIO'S WORDS

"Don't keep striving to find God. He is within you and with you, in your weeping and your seeking. He is like a mother who urges her little child to look for her, while she is behind him, and with her hands is vainly trying to make him come to her. I understand only too well the anguish of your state which is like the torments of hell. But don't worry or be frightened."[2]

"Do not let your heart be troubled in the hour of trial, because Jesus has promised His real assistance to those who follow Him. In times of struggle, remember Jesus; turn to Him and you will always be victorious. . . .

"Therefore, live tranquilly and don't be bewildered in the dark night through which your spirit is passing. Be patient and resigned while awaiting the return of your divine Sun who will soon come to brighten the forest of your spirit."[3]

PRAYER

Lord, I'll wait for You for as long as You want; You are *the Light. Amen.*

31

With Mother Mary and St. John

✠

From Psalm 31: "Into your hand I commit my spirit; you have redeemed me, O LORD, faithful God."[1]

God always rescues me, and yet I fear letting Him take complete charge.

ST. PIO'S WORDS

"You belong totally to Jesus. Therefore, let nothing detain you from abandoning yourself totally to the mercy of His Providence. Therefore, stay amidst the darkness of the passion. I say in the midst of this darkness, since this will enable you to consider the most-holy Virgin and St. John who, being at the foot of the cross amidst the frightening darkness, no longer heard nor saw our Lord, but felt nothing except grief and sadness. And even though they were animated with faith, this too was in darkness, as it was necessary for them to participate in the abandonment of our Lord. Consider yourself happy to be in such sweet company without understanding it."[2]

"By all means, continue to cry out with the Apostle Paul, 'I have been crucified with Christ,'[3] so that you will have to repeat, '. . . Father, into your hands I commend my spirit.'[4]"[5]

PRAYER

Help me to remain humble before You and to entrust my life to You.

32

In Christ's Sacred Heart

✠

From Psalm 32: "You are a hiding place for me."[1]

But does God really want me with all my afflictions?

ST. PIO'S WORDS

"The most afflicted souls are those who are closest to the divine Heart. And you can be sure that Jesus has chosen your soul as that which is most dear to His adorable Heart. You must hide yourself in this Heart; you must pour out your most ardent desires there, and in this Heart you must still live those remaining days which Providence grants you; you must die in this Heart when the Lord wishes.

"Without fully understanding it, you are hidden in this Heart. . . . In this Heart, you are, you live, and you move."[2]

"Don't ever fall back on yourself when the storm is raging. Place all your trust in the Heart of our most-sweet Jesus. . . . Renew your faith continually and never give it up, for faith never abandons anyone, much less a soul that is yearning to love God."[3]

PRAYER

I do love You, Lord. Always increase my love for You. Amen.

33

The Divine Bridegroom's "Kiss" of Love

✠

From Psalm 33: "The earth is full of the steadfast love of the LORD."[1]

If the earth is full of God's Love, then why do I see so much hatred all around me? Where can I go to find God's Love? Where?

ST. PIO'S WORDS

"Receive the Bread of angels [Holy Communion] with great faith and with a great flame of love in your heart. Await this most-tender Lover of your soul in order to be consoled in this life with the 'kiss' of His mouth. Happy are you if you succeed in receiving from the Lord the consolation of this 'kiss' in the present life! Then indeed will you feel your will inseparably bound at all times to Jesus' will."[2]

"In spirit, cling tightly all the time, to the divine will, then be at peace and serve the Lord with a joyful heart, for divine love will never grow less in your soul. . . . Continue to have boundless trust in the divine Mercy. I assure you that God loves you very much."[3]

". . . Say to God, 'Yes, oh divine Lover, Lord of my life, Your love is better than wine.'[4]"[5]

PRAYER

Help me to regularly receive You — and Your "kiss" — in the Eucharist.

34
Angel of the Lord

✠

From Psalm 34: "The angel of the LORD encamps around those who fear him, and delivers them."[1]

Is it true, a holy angel watches over me?

ST. PIO'S WORDS

"How consoling it is to know you are always under the protection of a heavenly spirit who never abandons you, not even when you are actually offending God. How delightful is this great truth to the one who believes! Who is to be feared, then, by the devout soul who is trying to love Jesus, when accompanied by such an illustrious warrior? . . .

"This good angel is praying for you and offers to God all your good works and your holy and worthy desires. When it seems to you that you are alone and abandoned, don't complain that you are without a friend to whom you can open your heart and confide your woes. For goodness sake, don't forget this invisible companion who is always there to listen to you, always ready to console you.

"Oh, delightful intimacy, oh, blessed companionship!"[2]

PRAYER

Lord, please bless abundantly my faithful and good guardian angel.

35
Open Your Heart

✠

From Psalm 35: "O LORD, do not be far from me!"[1]

Will God be near me when I face my enemies?

ST. PIO'S WORDS

"Why are you so afraid of your adversary? Don't you know that Jesus is invariably with you, and that the enemy of souls has no power over those who have resolved to belong entirely to God? The more you are afraid, the safer you are, and the more lukewarm you feel, the more secure you are."[2]

"Take your mind off disturbing and tormenting thoughts. Open your heart with boundless confidence to the only One who is able to console and save you. Have no fear for the future, for God is with you, and He is supremely faithful and will not allow you to be overwhelmed by your enemies. This divine Lover will never allow a soul that is consecrated to Him in a most-particular way to remain a victim of its enemies. No, no. The enemy will never obtain this victory."[3]

"May the grace and mercy and peace of our Lord Jesus Christ be with you always."[4]

PRAYER

Thank You for always protecting me. I love You, Lord.

36
Consider Jesus' Love for You

✠

From Psalm 36: "How precious is your steadfast love, O God!"[1]

I wish I could fully appreciate God's unfailing love for miserable me.

ST. PIO'S WORDS

"Consider Jesus' love for you and His concern for your well-being, and then be at peace. Do not doubt that He will invariably assist you with fatherly care against all your enemies. If He left it up to you to remain on your feet, you would never be able to do it. At the first breath of air, you would fall down and have no hope of rising again. The more numerous your enemies become, the more you should abandon yourself with complete trust in the Lord. He will always sustain you with His powerful arm so that you may not stumble. Before the Lord could abandon you, you would first have to close the door of your heart to Him. Even then, how many times does He not stretch out His hand to arrest your headlong dash toward the precipice? How many times, when you have abandoned Him, has He readmitted you to His loving embrace? How good God is! Blessed forever be His hand which many times alleviates your sufferings and heals your wounds."[2]

PRAYER

Lord, please always keep Your loving hand on me. Thank You. Amen.

37

Grace of Stillness, Grace of Silence

✠

From Psalm 37: "Be still before the LORD."[1]

But how can I be still, be silent, when noise and chaos surround me?

ST. PIO'S WORDS

"Try to withdraw, when possible; and in the silence of your heart; and in solitude, offer your praises and blessings, your contrite and humble heart, and your entire self to the heavenly Father. Thus, while the goodness of the divine Spouse is forgotten by the majority of His people . . . you must remain always close to Him by these periods of withdrawal. . . ."[2]

"Silently adore the divine disposition."[3]

"Lovingly humble yourself before God and people because God speaks to the humble. Love silence because much talk is never without sin.[4] Withdraw into yourself as much as you can, because in this way the Lord speaks freely to your soul, and your soul can listen to His voice."[5]

"I wish you, from the dear Redeemer, the grace of steadfastness of purpose, and especially that of being silent and letting everything around you be silent, in order to hear the voice of the Beloved."[6]

PRAYER

Lord, help me seek You in silence and there hear Your voice. Amen.

38

Do Not Be Afraid

✠

From Psalm 38: "O LORD, all my longing is known to you; my sighing is not hidden from you."[1]

I cry out to the Lord, but still I'm afraid.

ST. PIO'S WORDS

"As regards your spiritual state, I exhort you in the Lord not to be afraid, and in Him I reassure you. I want you to have greater trust in the divine Mercy. Humble yourself continually before the mercy of our God and invariably give thanks to Him for all the favors He has granted you. This attitude will be the most favorable for the reception of new graces which the heavenly Father, in His absolute love for you, intends to grant you. For, according to a principle of sound logic, those who fail to correspond with gratitude and continual untiring expressions of thanks for favors received are undeserving of further favors. Yes, trust in God and thank Him continually for everything, for in this way you will challenge and defeat all the anger of hell. I repeat: you are not to be afraid. The One who has helped you so far will continue His work of salvation."[2]

PRAYER

Thank You for all You have done, are doing, and will do for me. Amen.

39

To Live Is Christ, To Die Is Gain

✠

From Psalm 39: "LORD, let me know my end, and what is the measure of my days; let me know how fleeting my life is."[1]

If life is so short and so hard, why do we live at all?

ST. PIO'S WORDS

"Why do we live at all? As a result of your consecration at baptism, you belong to Jesus Christ. Hence, you should be familiar with this saying of St. Paul: 'For to me, living is Christ and dying is gain.'[2] [You must] live for Christ, live for His glory, live to serve Him, live to love Him. And when God wants to take your life from you, your sentiments and feelings should be those of a person who, at the end of his toil, goes to collect his wages. . . .

"All those who love God are ready for anything for love of that same God, in the hope that all will work out for their good. Always be prepared to recognize in every event of life the most-wise order of divine Providence. Adore it and conform your will in all things at all times to the will of God. In this way you shall give glory to the heavenly Father, and everything will be to your advantage for eternal life."[3]

PRAYER

Lord, help me believe that all *things will work to my good. Amen.*

40

Source of Inner Strength

✠

From Psalm 40: "I delight to do your will, O my God; your law is within my heart."[1]

Yes, God's commandments are in my heart, and I want to do God's will at all times, but from where can I get the inner strength to do so?

ST. PIO'S WORDS

"Eternal Father, how could I fulfill that petition made by Your Son for us, 'Your will be done, on earth as it is in heaven,'[2] if I did not receive strength from the Immaculate Flesh [in Holy Communion]? Even now, with the powerful help which Jesus has left us in this Sacrament of Love, I often feel I am on the point of wavering and rebelling against Your will. . . .

"Holy Father, 'Give us this day our daily bread [the Eucharist].'[3] Father, give us Jesus always during our brief stay in this land of exile. Give Him to us, and grant that we may be increasingly worthy to welcome Him into our hearts. Yes, give Him to us, and we shall be sure to fulfill the request that Jesus Himself addressed to You on our behalf: 'Your will be done, on earth as it is in heaven.'[4]"[5]

PRAYER

Father, give me Jesus, so that I will always do Your will. Amen.

41
Your Anchor

✠

From Psalm 41: "My enemies wonder in malice when I will die.... All who hate me whisper together about me; they imagine the worst for me."[1]

The enemy tells me I'm a fool to put all my hope in God.

ST. PIO'S WORDS

"I exhort you to be trustful. A soul who trusts in the Lord and places all its hopes in Him has nothing to fear. The enemies of your salvation are always around to snatch from your heart the anchor, your trust in God our Father, which is to lead you to salvation. Keep a very firm hold on this anchor and do not relinquish it for a moment. Otherwise all will be lost."[2]

"Always be on your guard and don't consider yourself to be good in any way, or above others. Don't imagine that you are better than they or at least as good, but consider all to be better than yourself. The enemy overcomes the arrogant and not the humble of heart. Drive away what the enemy is whispering loudly in your ear when he wants you to believe you are almost on the point of being lost. Despise these evil insinuations and live in peace, for the Lord is with you, as never before, in your tribulations."[3]

PRAYER

Lord, even when my enemies say that all is lost, I'll trust in You. Amen.

42
Unquenchable Thirst

✠

From Psalm 42: "As a deer longs for flowing streams, so my soul longs for you, O God. My soul thirsts for God, for the living God."[1]

I continually seek God, but He seems so far away.

ST. PIO'S WORDS

"How is it possible that the fountain of living water which issues from the divine Heart should be far from a soul that rushes to it like a thirsty deer? It is true that this soul may also fail to believe it because it feels continually consumed by an unquenchable thirst. But what of that? Does this, perhaps, go to show that the soul does not possess God? No, quite the opposite.

"This happens because the soul has not yet reached the end of its journey and is not yet totally immersed in the eternal fountain of His divine Love, which will happen in the kingdom of glory. Therefore . . . [drink] at this fountain of living water and go forward all the time along the way of divine love. . . . Be convinced that your soul will never be satisfied here below. In fact, it would be disastrous if you were to feel satisfied, for it would mean you thought you had reached your goal, and in this you would be deceived."[2]

PRAYER

Lord, thank You for the promise of eternal life with You. Amen.

43
Christt the Eternal Sun

✠

From Psalm 43: "O send out your light and your truth; let them lead me."[1]

Where is God when darkness surrounds my soul and I fear being lost?

ST. PIO'S WORDS

"Don't be bewildered if the night becomes deeper and darker for you. Don't be frightened if you are unable to see, with the eyes of the body, the serene sky that surrounds your soul. But look above, elevating yourself above yourself, and you will see a light that participates in the light of the eternal sun. A lively faith, blind belief, and complete adherence to the authorities appointed by God over you, this is the light that illuminated the steps of the people of God in the desert... the light that led the Magi to adore the newly born Messiah.... And this light also illuminates your soul and directs your footsteps so that you do not stumble."[2]

"Believe that the light shines in your soul.... Jesus, Sun of justice, is with you, loves you, and will always love you, given that you consent to His working freely within you."[3]

PRAYER

Lord, I do consent to Your working freely within me. Thank You. Amen.

44
Is God Sleeping?

✠

From Psalm 44: "Rouse yourself! Why do you sleep, O LORD?"[1]

When my life is a stormy sea, I fear God has forgotten me and is sleeping.

ST. PIO'S WORDS

"Stay in the boat in which our Lord has placed you and let the storms come. You will not perish. It appears to you that Jesus is sleeping, but let it be so. Don't you know that if He sleeps, His Heart vigilantly watches over you? Let Him sleep, but at the right time, He will awaken to restore your calm. Dearest St. Peter was frightened, and, beginning to sink, he exclaimed, 'Oh, Lord, save me!' And Jesus, taking him by the hand, replied, 'You of little faith, why did you doubt?'[2] Observe St. Peter. He walks with dry feet on the water; the waves and winds do not submerge him, but the *fear* of the waves and winds discourages and disheartens him. Fear is an evil worse than the evil itself.

"What do you fear? Isn't He watching over you? . . . But if fear takes you by surprise, cry out, 'Oh, Lord, save me!' He will stretch out His hand to you; hold onto it tightly, and joyfully walk on the stormy sea of life."[3]

PRAYER

Lord, even when the way seems dark, I will cling to You. Amen.

45

Mary Our Mother, Mary Our Queen

☩

From Psalm 45: "At your right hand stands the queen in gold."[1]

Who is this Queen of heaven and earth? How should I think about this Mother of our Lord Jesus Christ?

ST. PIO'S WORDS

"Reflect upon and keep before your mental gaze the great humility of the Mother of God, our Mother. The more she was filled with heavenly gifts, the more deeply did she humble herself, so that she was able to say, when overshadowed by the Holy Spirit who made her the Mother of God's Son, 'Here am I, the servant of the Lord.'[2] This dear Mother of ours was to break forth with the same words in the home of St. Elizabeth, although Mary bore in her chaste womb the Word Incarnate.[3] As gifts increase in you, let your humility grow, for you must consider that everything is given to you on loan."[4]

"May Mary be the star which shines on your path, and may she show you the safe way to reach the heavenly Father. May she be like an anchor to which you must be more closely attached in the time of trial."[5]

PRAYER

Lord, thank You for so great a Mother who leads us to You. Amen.

46
Wait for the Heavenly Roar

✠

From Psalm 46: "Be still, and know that I am God!"[1]

In this noisy, hectic world, how can I be still, be quiet before God?

ST. PIO'S WORDS

"To succeed better in prayer, remember that graces and enjoyment of prayer are not waters of this earth, but of heaven, and therefore all your efforts are not enough to let them fall. . . . Be diligent in praying, but at the same time humble and tranquil. Keep your heart open towards heaven and await the heavenly roar from there. . . . Through this, you will move closer to God, and you will place yourself in His presence for two reasons. The first is to render God the honor and consideration you owe Him, and this can be done without Him speaking to you or you speaking to Him. This obligation is paid by your recognizing Him as your God and you as His creature, spiritually prostrate in His presence, without His speaking to you."[2]

". . . Wait for God to speak to you. One day He will pronounce words of peace and consolation to you, and then you will know that your suffering served a good purpose and your patience was useful."[3]

PRAYER

Lord, help me to adore You in silence, whenever possible. Amen.

47

My Soul Magnifies the Lord

✠

From Psalm 47: "For the LORD, the Most High, is awesome, a great king over all the earth."[1]

In His infinite glory, why would God bother with miserable, finite me?

ST. PIO'S WORDS

"May Jesus be blessed forever, that, in the midst of a corrupt nation, He desired to draw you to His love.... May you exult and triumph, because there are other people, too, who know of His goodness and infinite perfection.... Spend your life giving thanks to the divine Father who, in an excess of love for you, sent His only begotten Son and our most-sweet Lover! Protected, covered, and defended by this dear Lord, stand before Him and pray with the humility of the creature and the confidence and freedom of a child. And given that He loves to delight in you, let nothing in the world distract you from delighting in Him as you contemplate His grandeur and infinite titles.... Pray to Him that He be generous with His divine help so that ... you, too, can say in truth, with our heavenly Mother, 'My soul magnifies the Lord, and my spirit rejoices in God my Savior.'[2]"[3]

PRAYER

Lord, may Your Mother always help me to praise You and rejoice. Amen.

48
Your Divine Guide

✠

From Psalm 48: "He will be our guide forever."[1]

Why does God choose to lead me along such rough paths?

ST. PIO'S WORDS

"I implore you in the most-sweet Lord to pay little attention to the path on which the Lord places you in order that you arrive at the promised land, paradise. . . . I exhort you, by the meekness of Jesus, to keep your eyes always fixed on Him who guides you, and on the heavenly homeland to which He wants to lead you. Why should you worry whether Jesus wants you to reach the homeland by way of the desert or through fields, when one way or the other, you will reach blessed eternity just the same?"[2]

"Follow Jesus along the path of suffering. Keep your gaze fixed on heaven, and all difficulties on your journey will be happily overcome."[3]

"Happy are you who, contrary to your merit, are already on the hill of Calvary by the divine Mercy. You have already been made worthy to follow the heavenly Master."[4]

"May the divine grace be your guide and sustenance in everything."[5]

PRAYER

No matter how rough the path, Lord, I will follow You. Amen.

49
You Can't Take It With You

✝

From Psalm 49: "When [the rich] die they will carry nothing away."[1]

But still I worry a lot about earthly, material needs.

ST. PIO'S WORDS

"Baptism brings about a real transformation in you. You die to sin and are grafted onto Jesus Christ in such a way as to live by His very life. . . . Now if baptism causes you to die to the first life and rise up to the second, it is your duty to seek the things of heaven and not to care about the things of this world. St. Paul says, 'Set your mind on things that are above, not on things that are on earth, for you have died, and your life is hidden with Christ in God.'[2]

". . . At baptism you are lifted up to a supernatural life and acquire the splendid hope of occupying a heavenly throne in glory. . . . Your vocation demands that you aspire continually to reach heaven and consider yourself to be a pilgrim in this land of exile. . . . Do not attach your heart to this miserable world. . . . Despise all things which do not help you to obtain what is eternal."[3]

PRAYER

Lord, please grant the grace of detachment from worldly things. Amen.

50

Heavenly Benefactor

✠

From Psalm 50: "Offer to God a sacrifice of thanksgiving."[1]

Too often I fail to thank God for His countless blessings.

ST. PIO'S WORDS

"The knowledge of God's plan for you must serve, on the one hand, to arouse gratitude in the depths of your soul towards so good a Father, so that you may give continual and heartfelt thanks to your heavenly Benefactor. Unite your praise to that of the Most Holy and Immaculate Mary, of the angels, and of all the blessed inhabitants of the heavenly Jerusalem."[2]

"Remain in an attitude of humility before the infinite goodness of the Lord. Open your heart all the time and give thanks uninterruptedly to the good God for the favors He is continually showering upon you, for the person who fails to be grateful for favors already received is unworthy to receive further graces. Let the divine grace act freely within you. Make use of it always for His glory and for your salvation and that of all other souls."[3]

"Infinite praise and thanks to Jesus, King of souls, for treating you as a chosen child of His own."[4]

PRAYER

I will spend my life thanking and praising You, Lord. Amen.

51

Divine Doctor

✠

From Psalm 51: "Do not take your holy spirit from me."[1]

I'm too imperfect and prone to sin for the Holy Spirit to dwell in me.

ST. PIO'S WORDS

"Religion is the academy of perfection in which each soul must learn to allow itself to be handled, planed, and smoothed by the divine Spirit, when He also acts as the Doctor of our souls so that, having been well-planed and smoothed, we can be united and joined to the will of God.

"The sign of perfection is that of being submitted to the divine will in the trials of the spirit. Religion is a hospital for the spiritually ill who wish to be cured, and in order to achieve this, they submit themselves to bleeding, probing, surgical instruments, fire, and all the pains of medicine.

" . . . In order to be healed spiritually, try to be healed perfectly. And in order to be healed, desire to bear the treatment and correction of the divine Doctor, and beseech Him not to spare you in anything in order to save you."[2]

"May the Holy Spirit always fill your heart with all the grace it can contain; may He fortify and sanctify you."[3]

PRAYER

Father, please fill me with Your Spirit and sanctify me, a sinner. Amen.

52

In the Olive Grove

✠

From Psalm 52: "I trust in the steadfast love of God forever and ever."[1]

But what if God withdraws His love from me?

ST. PIO'S WORDS

"Carry on tranquilly, for the divine Mercy will not be lacking, and much less will it be lacking in your case, if you show docility beneath the Lord's divine action. Don't be stingy with this heavenly Physician. For pity's sake, don't keep Him waiting any longer. To you He is saying, 'My child, give me your heart,[2] so that I may pour my oil into it.' . . . Open the door of your heart to Him with trustful abandonment. Don't hold up the precious stream of His oil as it is poured upon you, lest you have to go in search of this oil of His Mercy at the hour of death like the foolish virgins of the Gospel, for you will then find nobody willing to give it to you.[3] Yes, during life, always remain united with Jesus in the olive grove as He suffers His agony. By sharing thus in the anointing of His grace and the comfort of His strength, you will find yourself, after death, among the same olive trees to share in the joy of His ascension and His glory."[4]

PRAYER

Lord, I open my heart to You. Do with me as You will. Amen.

53
Weak, Yet Strong

✠

From Psalm 53: "For God will scatter the bones of the ungodly; they will be put to shame, for God has rejected them."[1]

God may have rejected them, but my enemies are still stronger than I am.

ST. PIO'S WORDS

"You feel weak in the face of this strong enemy of yours. Well, take comfort in our most-sweet Lord, because the soul's greatest misery is when it does not feel weak, but feels strong; when it trusts in itself [instead of God]. If all souls experienced this holy weakness, we would not see so many souls fall. A soul who felt its weakness and had recourse to God for help has never fallen. The soul is only defeated when, trusting in what it believes to be its abundant strength, thinks it can always sustain and bear temptations. Out of presumption . . . the soul finds itself falling right to the doors of hell.

" . . . Don't lose heart at the weakness you feel, because the soul that fears does not trust itself, but stays awake and prays, because of its weakness, and thus it becomes strong. But as happens to those who trust in themselves, as if they were a God, they soon experience their miseries and weakness."[2]

PRAYER

Lord, please always be my Strength because I am always so weak. Amen.

54
Do Not Torment Yourself

✠

From Psalm 54: "Save me, O God."[1]

Sometimes I wonder if I will ever get to heaven.

ST. PIO'S WORDS

"Oh how burdensome this mortal life is to the children of God! But the next life, which the mercy of the Lord will be pleased to grant you, will be more than you can desire. You certainly must not doubt your possessing it one day, even though you are sinful; and if you are not so sinful, it is simply because God is merciful toward those who place all their hope in Him. . . .

"When you find yourself exposed to some trial — either physical or moral, in body or in spirit — the best remedy is to think of Him who is your life. . . . I beg you not to examine whether your past, present, or future actions were, are, or will be too small, or if they were done well or badly. Merely abstain from sin and from those actions which you clearly see to be sinful, and do all with an upright conscience and with the will to please God."[2]

"Walk with simplicity in the ways of the Lord and do not torment yourself."[3]

PRAYER

I promise to avoid sin and try to do everything to please You. Amen.

55
The Ever-Present Grace

＋

From Psalm 55: "I am troubled in my complaint. I am distraught by the noise of the enemy."[1]

I worry because the enemy tells me I always offend God.

ST. PIO'S WORDS

"Do not listen to what your imagination and the enemy suggest to you. They would like you to believe that you are continually offending God and that you always, or nearly always, resist the divine call. The ever-present grace of the heavenly Father keeps you quite far from falling into such infidelities. Be quite sure of this. Those negative thoughts come from nowhere else than your own imagination and the evil one. Be careful not to attach any importance to them; their only purpose is to cool your feelings of affection toward your heavenly Spouse, and to make Christian perfection appear irksome by representing it as difficult and impossible for you to attain. Worse still, your imagination and the enemy aim more directly at drying up and causing to wither every sentiment of devotion in your heart."[2]

"May the peace of Jesus Christ be in your heart."[3]

PRAYER

Lord, thank You for the grace and mercy to attain perfection. Amen.

56
God's Bottle of Tears

✠

From Psalm 56: "You have kept count of my tossings; put my tears in your bottle."[1]

It grieves me to see so many people deep in habitual sin.

ST. PIO'S WORDS

"You are distressed by people's ingratitude toward God, and you do well to weep over their misfortunes. In reparation to God, offer Him your blessing and all your actions, making sure that all of these are good. But after you have wept privately over the misfortunes of others, it is well to imitate once more our Lord and the apostles by dismissing these things from your mind and turning to other matters and other occupations more useful for God's glory and the salvation of souls. . . .

"To spend too much time in deploring the state of those who obstinately persist in sinning would be a waste of time which could be appropriately spent, and should be spent, in promoting the salvation of others and in works for God's glory."[2]

"Don't worry about anything."[3]

PRAYER

By Your grace, I won't worry; I'll work and do all for Your glory. Amen.

57

When Storms Circle Around You

✠

From Psalm 57: "In the shadow of your wings I will take refuge, until the destroying storms pass by."[1]

When storms batter my heart and soul, fear also attacks.

ST. PIO'S WORDS

"Do not fear the storm that roars around your spirit, because in accordance with the severity of the winter, the spring will be equally more or less beautiful and rich with flowers, and the harvest equally more or less abundant."[2]

"May Jesus console your spirit which is tossed about in the stormy sea. But do not be afraid, because the storm that surrounds your spirit will calm down, and you will not be submerged. The little ship of your spirit always has the strong anchor of trust in the divine goodness."[3]

"Keep cheerful and don't be discouraged. The temptations and storms that are circling around you are sure signs that God favors you. Your fear of offending God is the surest proof that you are not offending Him."[4]

"May Jesus always rest His gaze on you and console your spirit which is so tossed about in the stormy sea. Amen."[5]

PRAYER

Lord, thank You even for "storms"; they propel me into Your arms. Amen.

58

Do Not Be Surprised

✠

From Psalm 58: "Do you indeed decree what is right, you [evil ones]? . . . No, in your hearts you devise wrongs."[1]

It seems as if the world tries to trick me into doing wrong and sinning.

ST. PIO'S WORDS

"Despise always the evil tricks of your enemy who is trying to arouse in you a feeling of horror. He is the enemy of everything that is good; therefore you must not be surprised if he fumes with rage. . . .

"To all appearances, this ugly scoundrel wanted and wants to play tricks on you. But trust in the Lord that you, with His powerful help, will rid yourself of the enemy. . . . That vile and evil one, envious of the good of others, a liar and deceiver, might take further revenge on you. But do not fear because, with divine help, he will be weakened. . . . Don't listen to the enemy; never dwell on his suggestions; despise him and beware of stopping to converse directly with him."[2]

"Don't lose heart; Jesus is always at your side. He will always fight with you and for you and, as always, the enemy will be completely defeated."[3]

PRAYER

Lord, with You by my side, no evil can control me. Thank You. Amen.

59

Powerful Help of Divine Paternal Love

From Psalm 59: "But I will sing of your might."[1]

It's hard to sing God's praises when He seems so far away.

ST. PIO'S WORDS

"Jesus is with you, and where He is, the kingdom of God is found. Your continual aspiring to Him should convince you of this. Can Jesus possibly be far from you when you call to Him, pray to Him, seek Him? How is it possible for divine love to be lacking in you, when you, like a deer parched with thirst,[2] hasten to that eternal source of living water? . . .

"Lift up your heart. Do not become discouraged in the face of the trials to which the divine Mercy wishes to subject you. He wants to test and strengthen you once again at the school of sacrifice and suffering. . . . Pray with humility, and remember the calm after the rain; after the darkness, the light; after the storm and the turmoil, the placid quiet. The powerful help of the paternal love of God, and the great gifts of His divine Majesty, will undoubtedly crown your trust and perseverance with glory."[3]

PRAYER

Even in the middle of my troubles, please help me to sing Your praises. Remind me that Your peace always follows the turmoil. Amen.

60

Enormous Miracle

✠

From Psalm 60: "Have you not rejected us, O God?"[1]

Because of my sinfulness, God should, indeed, reject me.

ST. PIO'S WORDS

"Our justification by God is such an enormous miracle that sacred Scripture compares it to the resurrection of Jesus.[2] In converting us from ungodliness, God revealed His power more fully in our justification than in making heaven and earth from nothing, since there is a greater contrast between the sinner and grace than there is between nonexistence and being. Nonexistence is less far from God than is the sinner. Since nonexistence is the lack of being, it has no power to resist God's will, while the sinner as a being — and a *free* being — is capable of resisting all of God's wishes. . . .

"If only all people could understand the extreme wretchedness and dishonor from which God's omnipotent hand has rescued us. If we could only perceive that which still amazes the heavenly spirits, namely, the state to which God's grace has raised us, to be nothing less than His own children, destined to reign with His Son for all eternity!"[3]

PRAYER

Lord, thank You for Your miracle in saving me from sin. Amen.

61
With Eyes Fixed On High

✠

From Psalm 61: "Lead me to the rock that is higher than I."[1]

My problems threaten to pin me down and keep me there.

ST. PIO'S WORDS

"The struggle is certainly harsh and the blow painful, but keep your gaze fixed on high. . . . Take heart. Jesus makes you hear the same voice He allowed St. Paul to hear, ['My grace is sufficient for you, for power is made perfect in weakness.'][2] Fight valiantly and you will obtain the reward of strong souls. Never abandon yourself to yourself. In times of great struggle and prostration, turn to prayer, trust in God, and you will never be overcome by temptation. If the Lord puts you to the test, know that He will not permit this to be beyond your strength.[3] If you are despised by the world, enjoy it, because they first hated the Author of Life, the divine Master. If you are harassed and afflicted with every kind of privation, temptation, and trial, raise your eyes on high and redouble your courage. The Lord is with you, and there is no reason to fear. Let the enemy wage war on you, but he will never be able to bite you. . . . Keep your gaze fixed on high."[4]

PRAYER

Thank You for not allowing problems to be more than I can bear. Amen.

62
Worldly Seductions

✠

From Psalm 62: "If riches increase, do not set your heart on them."[1]

But it's so hard to resist the seduction of earthly, material things.

ST. PIO'S WORDS

"Always struggle against the appetites of the flesh, against worldly vanity, against the seduction of gold or dignity, with which the evil one continually wages war on you."[2]

"How right you are to place your desire for the world in the hands of heavenly Providence, in order that your worldly desire might not vainly occupy your soul, as it would undoubtedly do if it were left to itself."[3]

"Practice internal and external sweetness a great deal, and maintain a tranquil heart amidst your multiple worries. . . . Continue to keep your soul raised on high, without looking upon this world, except to despise it, nor using your time, except to aspire to eternity."[4]

"May the sweet Jesus deign to make you such that, surrounded by the world and the flesh, you may live in the Spirit. . . . Praise Him with the angels, and may the foundation of your hope always be on high."[5]

PRAYER

Lord, please keep my body, mind, and soul fixed on high, on You. Amen.

63
Spiritual Dryness

✠

From Psalm 63: "My soul thirsts for you; my flesh faints for you, as in a dry and weary land where there is no water."[1]

Exhausted from work and worries, I seek God, but I can't find Him.

ST. PIO'S WORDS

"Don't be discouraged if you experience spiritual dryness. This does not mean the Lord has abandoned you.... You are too dear to the Heart of Jesus, and all that is happening in your soul is due to the exquisiteness of Jesus' love for you. He wants you entirely for Himself. He wants you to place all your trust and all your affection in Him alone, and it is for this reason that He sends you this spiritual aridity, to unite you more closely to Him, to rid you of certain little attachments which do not appear as such to you and which, in many cases, you do not even recognize or detect.

"... The state of your soul in such straits is a sad one because it seems to you that all is ended and that the Lord has left you forever.... Instead ... the Lord is never as pleased with you as He is at such a time as this.... Don't worry, then, because the Lord will ... never withdraw from you."[2]

PRAYER

Lord, I will trust Your loving presence, even if You seem far away. Amen.

64
Your Divine Guide to Christian Perfection

✠

From Psalm 64: "Because of their tongue he will bring them to ruin."[1]

I try to be kind in speech, but unkind words sometimes slip out.

ST. PIO'S WORDS

"Beware . . . you can offend others externally by your speech. This can happen especially in three ways: first, by blasphemy, either by rebelling against God in offensive terms, or against your neighbor by harsh, unpleasant words and curses. Second, by impure language which reveals the nasty fire that burns in the heart and that spreads and affects everyone else. Third, by lying. This gives birth to deceit, false testimony, and other evil deeds. . . . Beware of all of these if you intend to live according to the Spirit of Jesus Christ."[2]

"The Apostle Paul suggests two most-powerful means for the attainment of Christian perfection: the constant study of God's law and the performance of all our actions for His glory."[3]

"May the grace of the divine Spirit always reign supreme in your soul, and may He guide you to greater Christian perfection."[4]

PRAYER

Lord, by Your grace, I vow to say only kind things about others. Amen.

65
You Are Chosen

✠

From Psalm 65: "Happy are those whom you choose and bring near to live in your courts."[1]

God couldn't have chosen me; I struggle daily with temptations.

ST. PIO'S WORDS

"No chosen soul is free from temptations. Not even the Apostle Paul who, after being taken away to paradise while still a traveling soul, was subjected to such a trial that included the evil one hitting him. Dear God!"[2]

"You are certainly in the pit, but that of Daniel. You are certainly in the sepulcher, but that of our Lord. You descended there, not as a result of guilt, not as a punishment, but by the loving will of the heavenly Father, who treats you just as He treats His favorites who are predestined to be conformed to the image of His Son.[3] To fear in your state is like fearing in the arms of your mother. You do not offend God in that state, and what you believe [to be your countless sins], are merely semblances and representations, but not reality. This is the whole truth and nothing but the truth."[4]

PRAYER

Father, whatever it takes, conform me to Your Son's image. Amen.

66
Your Omnipotent God

✠

From Psalm 66: "Say to God, 'How awesome are your deeds! Because of your great power, your enemies cringe before you.'"[1]

Yes, God is awesome, but I still fear my enemies.

ST. PIO'S WORDS

"I rejoice with you in the Lord at the goodness this God is showing you. Fear nothing. God has total possession of your soul and is working within you in a marvelous manner. You need do nothing except expand your soul before so much goodness, and invite Him to work always powerfully within you. Let God shake you when and as He wishes . . . and all will work out for His greater glory and your perfection."[2]

"You imagine that your powerlessness damages you, and it seems to you that this powerlessness prevents you from withdrawing into yourself and from moving closer to God. This is a very great mistake because you suppose wrongly. God has placed you in that state for His glory and for your greater benefit. He wants your miseries to be the throne of His mercy, and your powerlessness the seat of His Omnipotence."[3]

PRAYER

Thank You for using my misery and weaknesses for Your glory. Amen.

67
Spirit of Joyfulness

✠

From Psalm 67: "Let the nations be glad and sing for joy."[1]

Why try to be glad and joyful when the world is in such a mess?

ST. PIO'S WORDS

"Preserve a spirit of holy joyfulness."[2]

"Nourish your soul with a spirit of cordial confidence in God. Increase your courage, and hope a great deal in accordance with the degree to which you find yourself surrounded by imperfections and miseries. Be very humble, as this is the virtue of virtues, but see that it is a generous and tranquil humility. Always be faithful in serving God well, but observe loving freedom in His service, without your heart feeling even the slightest drop of bitterness.

"Yes, preserve a spirit of holy joyfulness, which, being modestly spread throughout your actions and words, brings consolation to people, the children of God, so that they might glorify God for it, in accordance with the rule given to us by our divine Master....[3] Never permit your soul to become sad... because Jesus is the Spirit of sweetness and is completely lovable."[4]

PRAYER

Lord, for the sake of those around me, help me to be always joyful. Amen.

68
You're in the Book of Life

✠

From Psalm 68: "Our God is a God of salvation, and to God, the LORD, belongs escape from death."[1]

But what if I succumb to temptations and never gain eternal life?

ST. PIO'S WORDS

"Remember and keep well-impressed in your mind that Calvary is the hill of the saints. But remember also that after having climbed Calvary, the cross having been erected, and you having died on it, you immediately ascend another mount, Tabor [Mount of the Transfiguration]. Remember that the suffering is short-lived, but the reward is eternal. Rest tranquilly, or at least resignedly, always secure. . . . Trust in God's authority and do not fear the raging tempest because the little ship of your spirit will never be submerged. Heaven and earth will pass away, but the word of God assures you that whoever obeys will sing victory, will never pass away, but will always remain written indelibly in the Book of Life. You will always exist."[2]

"May Jesus be your comfort, sustenance, and compensation in this life and for blessed eternity."[3]

PRAYER

Please help me always obey You, so I can live forever with You. Amen.

69
Deep Waters

✠

From Psalm 69: "... I have come into deep waters, and the flood sweeps over me."[1]

Why do I feel abandoned by God in a sea of troubles?

ST. PIO'S WORDS

"Take heart because the Lord is with you. He suffers with you, groans with you, and is pleased with you. . . . Haven't you loved our Lord up until now? Don't you still love Him? Don't you yearn to love Him forever? Therefore, have no fear. Even if you were to have committed all the sins of this world, Jesus tells you, 'Your sins are forgiven.'[2] But then you will say to me, 'What is the reason for this trial of abandonment of my poor soul?' It is the trial of heavenly love. 'I have come into deep waters, and the flood sweeps over me.'[3] But then the prophet added, 'Do not let the flood sweep over me. . . .'[4] This is the trial of souls who are loved by Jesus who was pleased to experience all the fear of that moral tempest in the desert, in the Garden, and on Calvary. . . . Every predestined soul must resemble Jesus. . . . Therefore, let Him treat you as He pleases."[5]

PRAYER

Lord, thanks for forgiveness and love. Do with me as You will. Amen.

70
The Crown That Awaits You

✠

From Psalm 70: "But I am poor and needy; hasten to me, O God!"[1]

Does God really care that I'm "poor and needy" when undergoing trials?

ST. PIO'S WORDS

"I beg you to fear nothing as regards the needs of your soul. The terrible trials through which your soul is traversing are willed by God. They serve and will continue to serve for His glory and your sanctification. It is not vengeful justice, but it is the trial of every soul that has chosen Christ as its portion and inheritance. It is not vengeful justice that is treating you in this manner, but rather, the divine Father's love, who wishes to render you similar to his Son who in every respect has been tempted as you are, yet without sinning.[2] It is not vengeful justice, but the trials of the soul called to complete what is lacking in the passion of Jesus Christ for love of Christ's Body, the Church.[3]

"... Rejoice, therefore, on seeing yourself always more similar to the Victim who is Jesus Christ. Rejoice, therefore, because the crown that awaits you is beautiful."[4]

PRAYER

Lord, for the sake of others, I'll accept the trials You send me. Amen.

71

Heavenly Musician

✠

From Psalm 71: "Do not forsake me when my strength is spent."[1]

When trials and sufferings exhaust me, what should I do?

ST. PIO'S WORDS

"Don't lose heart; in your weakness, unite yourself more to Jesus."[2]

" . . . Prostrate your heart before Jesus and humbly say, 'Lord, have mercy because I am weak.' Then get up peacefully, calm yourself, and with holy indifference, carry on with your tasks.

"You must behave in those times of struggle as a violinist usually behaves. Whenever that poor person notices discordance, he neither breaks the string nor gives up playing the violin, but immediately lends his ear in order to discover from where the discordance comes. Then he patiently tightens or loosens the string accordingly.

"Well, then, you too behave this way. Don't become impatient at such wearisome matters [as your daily struggles]. . . . Humble yourself before God. Gently tighten or loosen the strings of your heart before the heavenly Musician, in order that He might reorganize the concert."[3]

PRAYER

I place myself in Your hands. Please organize my life's "concert." Amen.

72

Eternal Peace

✠

From Psalm 72: "In his days may righteousness flourish and peace abound."[1]

If my troubles weren't so great, I could have that peace.

ST. PIO'S WORDS

"Don't desire in the slightest to be freed from that trial. A soldier must achieve a lot in war before he desires it to end. We will never acquire perfect sweetness and love if it is not exercised in the midst of great dislike, opposition, and disgust. True peace does not consist in fighting, but in winning. Those who have been beaten no longer fight, and they don't have true peace.

"Take heart. You must therefore humble yourself greatly, seeing that you are not the master of yourself, but that you greatly love comfort and rest. Always keep Jesus present to your gaze. He did not come in order to rest Himself, nor for His spiritual or temporal comforts, but in order to fight, humble Himself, and die [in order to rise again and to one day bring you with Him into the eternal peace of heaven]."[2]

PRAYER

Lord, forgive my complaining. Make me more and more like You. Amen.

73
Divine Presence

✠

From Psalm 73: "But for me it is good to be near God."[1]

How can I grow closer and closer to God?

ST. PIO'S WORDS

"As soon as you are before God in the Blessed Sacrament, devoutly genuflect. Once you have found your place, kneel down and render the tribute of your presence and devotion to Jesus in the Blessed Sacrament. Confide all your needs to Him, along with those of others. Speak to Him with filial abandonment, give free rein to your heart, and give Him complete freedom to work in you as He thinks best."[2]

"On leaving the church, be recollected and calm. First, take your leave of Jesus in the Blessed Sacrament; ask His forgiveness for the shortcomings committed in His divine Presence; and do not leave Him without asking for and receiving his paternal blessings."[3]

"Fly in spirit before the tabernacle when you cannot go there with the body, and there express your desires. Pray to and embrace the Beloved of souls, better than if you had been able to receive Him in the Sacrament."[4]

PRAYER

Lord, thank You that I can "fly" to You in spirit. Amen.

74
Necessary Winter

✠

From Psalm 74: "You have fixed all the bounds of the earth; you made summer and winter."[1]

But why does the bitter, harsh "winter" of my soul have to come at all?

ST. PIO'S WORDS

"All the seasons of the year can be found in your soul. Sometimes you feel the winter of sterility, distraction, listlessness, and boredom; sometimes the dews of the month of May with the perfume of holy little flowers [good deeds and penance]. Sometimes you experience the colors of the desire to please God. Nothing remains but the autumn, which does not bear much fruit, but it often happens that, when the grain is threshed and the grapes crushed, you find that the harvest is greater than it had promised!

"You would like it to be eternally spring and summer, but these rotations are necessary, both internally and externally. Only in heaven will everything be spring as regards beauty; autumn as regards enjoyment; and summer as regards love. There will be no winter, but here winter is necessary in order to practice self-denial and beautiful little virtues."[2]

PRAYER

Lord, when winters of body and of soul batter me, I will trust You. Amen.

75
How Great This Humility

From Psalm 75: "I say to the boastful, 'Do not boast. . . .' it is God who executes judgment, putting down one and lifting up another."[1]

Why does it sometimes seem as if God "puts down" His own children?

ST. PIO'S WORDS

"Always be more humble and make yourself more humble, day by day, in your eyes. Dear God, how great this humility is! It is the true grandeur of the children of God! I exhort you to pray continually for this."[2]

"Live in this way: sweet and lovable toward all; humble, courageous, pure, and sincere in everything. What better desire could I have for you? Be like a little spiritual bee who takes nothing into his hive except honey and wax. May your home be entirely full of sweetness, peace, agreement, humility, and piety, and may your conversation be entirely heavenly."[3]

"Our Lord loves you, and He loves you tenderly. And if He doesn't allow you to feel the sweetness of this love, it is in order to render you more humble in your own eyes. However, don't let this stop you from having recourse to His holy benevolence with every confidence."[4]

PRAYER

Lord, when I can't "feel" Your love, I will trust in Your presence. Amen.

76
A Thorn in God's Side

┼

From Psalm 76: "The earth feared and was still when God rose up to establish judgment, to save all the oppressed of the earth."[1]

I know I'm just a thorn in God's side, and I'll never make it to heaven.

ST. PIO'S WORDS

"You are not the object of God's vengeance; you are not unworthy and deserving of rejection and condemnation. All that is happening to you is the effect of love. It is a trial, a vocation to co-redemption, and a cause of glory. It is a fact that all your anxiety and trepidation — created by the enemy who takes wicked delight in tormenting you — is permitted by the supreme Good for the above-mentioned purpose. Therefore, all your anxiety should disappear.

"To call yourself a thorn that torments the Lord, and to recognize your unworthiness as an obvious fact . . . is a lie; a scene presented to you in glowing colors by the skillful artist of darkness whose treachery is equal to his ability to enhance his picture by the bold use of light and shade. It is untrue that you offend the most-sweet Lord when you are tempted."[2]

PRAYER

Thank You for Your love that won't let me succumb to serious sin. Amen.

77

My God, My God, Why Have You Forsaken Me?

✠

From Psalm 77: "Has his steadfast love ceased forever? Are his promises at an end for all time?"[1]

The world seems headed for disasters of all kinds. Where is God? Where is His Love? Where is the help He promises me in His holy word?

ST. PIO'S WORDS

"You say you are anxious about the future, but don't you know that the Lord is with you always and that the enemy has no power over one who has resolved to belong entirely to Jesus? Moreover, isn't God good and faithful to the point of not permitting you to be tempted beyond your strength? [2]"[3]

"How can you fail to rejoice when you are involved in combats, knowing that every victory has a corresponding degree of glory? May this thought of eternal bliss with Jesus, and of being made similar to Him, encourage you and prevent you from yielding to temptations. Be urged onward by the example of Jesus Christ, who in every respect was tempted like you, yet did not sin.[4] He was even tempted until He could bear no more and cried out, 'My God, why have You forsaken me?'[5]"[6]

PRAYER

Lord, forgive me for doubting Your constant vigilance over me. Amen.

78
Your Daily Bread

✠

From Psalm 78: "He rained down on them manna to eat, and gave them the grain of heaven. Mortals ate of the bread of angels."[1]

What is this food angels eat? Do I need it too?

ST. PIO'S WORDS

"Never fail to eat the Food of the angels."[2]

"Well then, His immense love, that same love that induced Him to leave the bosom of His eternal Father in order to come to earth and take upon Himself our fragility and our debts and satisfy the divine Justice for us, found an admirable means in which He showed us His exceedingly great love for us. What means was this? Oh, for the love of heaven, let us understand what our good Master asked the Father immediately after He had offered our will to Him. In His own name and in ours, Jesus asked Him also, 'Give us this day our daily bread.'[3]

"But what bread is this? In Jesus' request here, failing a better interpretation, I recognize primarily the Eucharist. Oh, the exceeding humility of this Man-God!"[4]

PRAYER

Thanks for continually humbling Yourself so I might receive You. Amen.

79
Health of Your Soul

✝

From Psalm 79: "How long, O LORD? Will you be angry forever?"[1]

Is my spiritual suffering punishment from God?

ST. PIO'S WORDS

"Unfortunately, you are in a state of spiritual suffering, and you will have to suffer more. . . . But trust in and love the goodness of our God. You are suffering, but be comforted, because you are suffering with Jesus and for Jesus, and it is not a punishment, but rather a trial for the health of your soul.

"Convince yourself of this. I assure you of it on behalf of the Lord. Jesus is present in your suffering, precisely in the center of your heart. You are neither separated nor far from the love of this good God. You experience the delight of the thought of God, but you still suffer at being far from possessing Him totally, and at seeing Him offended by ungrateful people. But it cannot be otherwise. Whoever loves, suffers. This is the law of the traveling soul. Love which is not yet satisfied is a torment, but a most-sweet torment. You are experiencing this.

"Go forward without fear!"[2]

PRAYER

Lord, help me accept suffering as "trial for the health" of my soul. Amen.

80

Beseech the Divine Lover

✠

From Psalm 80: "Restore us, O God of hosts; let your face shine, that we may be saved."[1]

My sinfulness and weaknesses sometimes frighten me.

ST. PIO'S WORDS

"You tell me you are frightened by your malice, and you want to know what more you can do to rid yourself of it. Humble yourself before the Lord with complete confidence and don't be afraid, for no harm will come to you. Your malice, moreover, is not, as you think, of such a nature as to incur the displeasure of the divine Spouse. Beseech our divine Lover to free you from these excessive fears, which, instead of opening the heart to Jesus' love, tend to close it.

"Let the delightful thought console you that you are always in the presence of Jesus who sees and knows and weighs all your actions. You ought to rejoice at this thought, for all your actions are directed towards a good end. I assure you of this in God's name and ask you to let this assurance calm you."[2]

PRAYER

Lord, Your mercy, love, and constant presence are my delight. Amen.

81
Your Own Garden

✠

From Psalm 81: "I would feed you with the finest of the wheat."[1]

When I receive that "finest of wheat" in the Eucharist, with what desire and intention should I receive our Lord to show Him my love and gratitude?

ST. PIO'S WORDS

"The Holy Eucharist is a great means through which you can aspire to perfection. But you must receive it with the desire and intention of removing from your heart all that is displeasing to Him with whom you wish to dwell. Try to continually overcome yourself in your daily struggles, which the Lord presents to you. And extend these efforts also to the constant exercise of correcting your defects, acquiring virtue, and doing good works. . . .

"May this be your only desire, and be sure that God wants nothing else from you at the present. Therefore . . . do not scatter your seeds in the gardens of others, but cultivate your own garden. Do not desire to be anything but what you are; concentrate on perfecting yourself and on carrying the crosses, either small or large, that you will encounter on your journey to heaven."[2]

PRAYER

Through the Eucharist, help me carry my cross and perfect myself. Amen.

82
Led by Your Divine Spouse

✠

From Psalm 82: "Rescue the weak and the needy; deliver them from the hand of the wicked."[1]

Weak and needy, I try to please God, but still my enemies torment me.

ST. PIO'S WORDS

"The one who upsets and torments you is the evil one. The One who enlightens you is God. The soul that tends more and more to degrade and humble itself before its Lord, and at the same time is induced to suffer and bear all things with a view to winning the approval of its heavenly Spouse, cannot fail to recognize that all this comes from God. The soul's ardent and loving yearnings for its Lord are not and cannot be illusions. The grace of Jesus is the source of the beautiful things happening to you. You must allow your divine Spouse to act in you and to lead you by the paths He chooses.

"...What you must do is to thank the Lord and be very glad.... Unite your heart with the Heart of Jesus and be simple-hearted as He desires. Make an effort to reproduce in yourself Jesus' own simplicity, and keep your heart far from earthly concerns and the shrewdness of the flesh."[2]

PRAYER

Lord, consume my humble heart in the fire of Your heart's love. Amen.

83

To Reach the Throne of God

+

From Psalm 83: "Those who hate you have raised their heads."[1]

I see the evil approaching, but where is God?

ST. PIO'S WORDS

". . . God is with you and will never abandon you to the evil one's attacks. You are downcast because you think. . . you do not possess the gift of holy meditation and the presence of God. On the contrary, our merciful Lord, in spite of all your unworthiness, has adorned you with the gift of His holy love. For this, give glory to the most-tender heavenly Father.

"What are these laments of your soul. . . these holy desires to belong entirely to Jesus, to please Him in everything? What is . . . that longing. . . to fly away to the bosom of the heavenly Father and be transformed in Him?

"Are not all these impulses the effects of that love which Jesus poured into your heart. . . ? Is it within the power of mortals like us to formulate these desires? Certainly not. The human spirit, without the flame of divine love, tends to reach the level of the beasts, while the love of God raises it up so high, it can even reach to the throne of God."[2]

PRAYER

Lord, let Your love transform me into the person You want. Amen.

84
Your Remaining Years

✠

From Psalm 84: "I would rather be a doorkeeper in the house of my God than live in the tents of wickedness."[1]

But my enemies tell me to seek prestige, power, and wealth.

ST. PIO'S WORDS

"The prophet says, 'I have chosen a lowly position in the house of God, rather than to live in the tents of sinners.'[2] I am sure you want to know what the best 'lowly position' is, and I tell you it is that which you have not chosen for yourself, or that which is less welcome to you. Or to explain this better, that position toward which you feel no inclination, that position of your vocation or profession. Who will grant you the grace of loving your 'lowly position'? Nobody can do this except He who greatly loved His own people, so that, in order to preserve them, He willed to die. Enough!

"Be totally resigned in the hands of our Lord; give Him your remaining years and beg Him to fill them with preparations for a life which is pleasing to Him. . . . Empty your heart of other affections, except His chaste love."[3]

PRAYER

Lord, I give You my life. Use my remaining years to please You. Amen.

85

The Divine Kiss

✠

From Psalm 85: "Steadfast love and faithfulness will meet; righteousness and peace will kiss."[1]

How can I receive this "kiss" in the middle of my daily struggles?

ST. PIO'S WORDS

"With faith and hope you will arm yourself in order to sustain the struggle in which the heavenly Father's goodness has involved you. With faith and hope, you will not be without the sweet nectar of love, which unites you more and more to the supreme Good."[2]

"Remember that you are a child of a merciful Father who is indulgent toward you. If the Lord were to judge you according to strict justice, you would not be saved. So make righteousness and peace kiss,[3] by always practicing mercy rather than justice, in imitation of your heavenly Father."[4]

"In order to arrive at an heroic degree of love, which enables you to ask Jesus to favor you with a 'kiss' of His divine mouth, God's powerful assistance is required. Ask for and desire this powerful help by seeking God continually with the Spouse in the Song of Solomon."[5]

PRAYER

Lord, by Your grace, I will always seek You and practice mercy. Amen.

86
Thy Will Be Done

✠

From Psalm 86: "Teach me your way, O LORD, that I may walk in your truth."[1]

I do want to walk in God's truth, but I don't deserve such a grace, a gift.

ST. PIO'S WORDS

"I give heartfelt thanks to the heavenly Father, through His most beloved Son Jesus, for all the graces which He scattered and continually scatters in your soul, despite your unworthiness. How good the Lord is to everyone, but He is even more so to those who have a true and sincere desire to please Him in everything, and who fulfill the divine plan in themselves.

"You, too, must learn to more greatly recognize and adore the divine will in all the events of life. Often repeat the divine words of our dearest Master, 'Your will be done, on earth as it is in heaven.'[2] Let this beautiful exclamation always be in your heart and on your lips. . . . Say it in times of affliction; say it in times of temptation and during the trials to which Jesus wants to subject you. Say it again when you feel yourself submerged in the ocean of love for Jesus; it will be your anchor and salvation."[3]

PRAYER

Lord, in all circumstances, help me to say, "Thy will be done." Amen.

87

Heaven, the Eternal Tabernacle

✠

From Psalm 87: "Glorious things are spoken of you, O city of God."[1]

When my miseries consume me, I can't even imagine heaven's glory.

ST. PIO'S WORDS

". . . Paul was one of the greatest saints. . . . Yet he was persecuted, he suffered, he was tormented for love of Jesus Christ! . . . [Paul] experienced many revelations, visions, and ecstasies. He was even carried away to the 'third' heaven. And yet Paul, rich in virtues and excellent gifts . . . confesses his many vigils and fasts, having suffered hunger, thirst, nudity, and the rigors of the cold, and all of it tolerated for love of Jesus. Paul reveals having been carried away to paradise while still in mortal flesh.[2] He even reaches the point of saying, '. . . it is no longer I who live, but it is Christ who lives in me.'[3]"[4]

"May Jesus possess you and render you always more worthy of greater heights. . . . How happy you will be in this miserable life, because in this way, the end of it will be the beginning of a beautiful and holy eternity. . . . [God] will never abandon you until you are assured of His eternal tabernacle."[5]

PRAYER

Lord, thank You that, even in my misery, You never abandon me. Amen.

88
Superabundant Strength

✠

From Psalm 88: "For my soul is full of troubles, and my life draws near to [death]."[1]

The strength of my troubles sometimes seems deadly.

ST. PIO'S WORDS

"In order to reach the haven of salvation, the Holy Spirit tells us, the souls of the elect must pass through and be purified in the fire of painful humiliations, like gold and silver in the melting pot. In this way they are spared from atoning for their sins in the next life. 'Accept whatever befalls you, and in times of humiliation be patient. For gold is tested in the fire, and those found acceptable, in the furnace of humiliation.'[2]

"Jesus wants to make you holy at all costs, but above all He wants to sanctify you. He offers you continual proof of this; it would seem as if He had nothing else to do but sanctify your soul. Oh, how good Jesus is! The continual crosses to which He subjects you, giving you not merely the necessary strength, but super-abundant strength to bear them meritoriously, are most certain and singular signs of His deep love for you."[3]

PRAYER

Lord, use my crosses to make me holy and wholly for You. Amen.

89

Humiliations of Christ

✠

From Psalm 89: "All who pass by plunder him; he has become the scorn of his neighbors. You have exalted the right hand of his foes; you have made all his enemies rejoice."[1]

Why did God the Father allow people to seize, scorn, and crucify Jesus?

ST. PIO'S WORDS

"Consider how the Son of God abased Himself in His incarnation, His mortal life, and especially in His painful death. . . . It was this humiliation which led to His honor and glory, that by His example He confirmed His own words, '. . . Those who humble themselves will be exalted.'[2]

"Meditate every day on the humiliations of the Son of God and the glory to which they led. Consider how the divine Word abased Himself. As St. Paul says, 'For in him the whole fullness of deity dwells bodily. . . .'[3] Jesus Christ did not hesitate to lower Himself to our level in order to raise us up to fullness of life in God. Of His own free will and to the fullest extent, this divine Word was pleased to abase Himself to our level, by hiding His divine nature beneath the veil of human flesh."[4]

PRAYER

Lord, "hide" Yourself in me; keep me humble, like You. Amen.

90
Joys of Eternity

✠

From Psalm 90: "Make us glad as many days as you have afflicted us, and as many years as we have seen evil."[1]

But I need to be "glad" and comforted now, when I am afflicted.

ST. PIO'S WORDS

"Let it be a consolation to you to know that the joys of eternity will be all the more heartfelt and profound, the more numerous the days of humiliation and the years of unhappiness you have known in the present life. This is not just my own opinion, for Holy Scripture offers you infallible testimony to this effect. The psalmist says, 'Make us glad as many days as you have afflicted us, and as many years as we have seen evil.'[2] St. Paul says in his letter to the Corinthians that a moment of our passing trials can win for us unimaginable glory in eternity.[3]"

"Calm the tormenting anxieties of your heart and banish all those distressing thoughts which are all suggested by the evil one in order to make you act badly. Jesus is always with you, even when you don't feel His presence. . . . He is there to ward off the enemy's blows."[4]

PRAYER

Lord, help me to let go of my anxieties and to trust in You. Amen.

91
Your Angelic Brother

✠

From Psalm 91: "For he will command his angels concerning you to guard you in all your ways. On their hands they will bear you up, so that you will not dash your foot against a stone."[1]

With trouble always ready to defeat me, I need a good, holy angel's help.

ST. PIO'S WORDS

"May your good guardian angel always watch over you; may he be your guide on the bitter paths of life. May he always keep you in the grace of Jesus and sustain you with his hands so that you may not stumble on a stone. May he protect you under his wings from all the snares of the world, the evil one, and the flesh. Have great devotion to this good angel. How consoling it is to know that near you is a spirit who, from the cradle to the tomb, does not leave you even for an instant, not even when you dare to sin. And this heavenly spirit guides and protects you like a friend, a brother. . . . Your angel prays without ceasing for you."[2]

"May your good angel remain watchful by your side; may he protect you and support you with his hands, lest you dash your foot against a stone."[3]

PRAYER

Lord, Your mercy and love astound me. Thank You for my angel. Amen.

92
Thank Your Most-Tender Spouse

✠

From Psalm 92: "It is good to give thanks to the LORD."[1]

It's tough to thank God when I'm discouraged and suffering.

ST. PIO'S WORDS

"Humble yourself before God, rather than become discouraged if the heavenly Father reserves the suffering of His Son for you. In His holy Humanity, God permitted Him to be tempted by the evil one three times.[2] You must elevate prayers of hope and resignation to Him and sing a hymn of recognition, praise, and thanksgiving."[3]

"Forget your doubts. Calm your anxiety, and humble yourself always more before the goodness of our God, never ceasing to thank Him for the continual favors He bestows on you and on many other souls."[4]

"Render heartfelt thanks to your most-tender Spouse. Contrary to your every merit, you are on the steps of Tabor [Mount of the Transfiguration], by having a firm determination to love and serve His divine goodness well. Therefore, you must have great hope. . . . Ascend without tiring to the heavenly vision of the Savior."[5]

PRAYER

Lord, keep me on Your "straight and narrow" path. Amen.

93
King of Your Heart

✢

From Psalm 93: "The LORD is king, he is robed in majesty; the LORD is robed, he is girded with strength."[1]

Where is this strength and majesty when misfortune makes me bitter?

ST. PIO'S WORDS

"Practice holy sweetness in all misfortunes which often present themselves in this life. Be tranquil and at peace, always keeping our Lord in your heart. How happy you will be if you are steadfast in the hands of the divine Majesty, amid your worries and your daily tasks, which will be extremely pleasant because God will help you. And the slightest consolation you feel will be greater than any the world could give you."[2]

"May Jesus continue to be the King of your heart! I say 'may He continue' because He is such already, and it should console you in the terrible trials through which your soul is passing. Be quite resigned, and if possible, at peace. . . ."[3]

". . . as long as your most-sweet God reigns within you, and He will reign there eternally; have no fear."[4]

PRAYER

Lord, be King of my heart and sweeten me with Your sweetness. Amen.

94

Groaning of the Heart

✠

From Psalm 94: "For the LORD will not forsake his people; he will not abandon his heritage."[1]

At times, it certainly feels *as if God has abandoned me.*

ST. PIO'S WORDS

"Oh God! Oh God! Do not allow your inheritance to be lost. Oh God! Let Yourself always be heard more and more by my poor heart, and accomplish in me the work You have begun."[2]

"You know, oh Lord, of the warm tears I have shed before You during extremely grievous times. You know, God of my soul, of the groanings of my heart, the tears that descended from my eyes. You had the unquestionable sign of those tears and of the battle I was fighting, from the pillows that remained soaked with them. I always wanted to obey You. . . . I wanted to die, rather than fail in Your calling. But You, oh Lord . . . arose in the end; You held out your powerful hand to me and led me to where you had first called me. Oh my God, may infinite praise and thanks be rendered to You."[3]

PRAYER

Lord, thanks for never letting me go, even when my heart groans. Amen.

95

In the Presence of God

+

From Psalm 95: "Let us come into his presence with thanksgiving."[1]

Life's so hectic, I seldom have time to acknowledge His presence.

ST. PIO'S WORDS

"Take care not to lose the presence of God by any action whatsoever. Never undertake any work or action without first raising your mind to God and directing to Him, with a pure intention, the action you are about to perform. You should do likewise at the end of every action.

"Examine yourself as to whether you have done everything with the right intention you had at the beginning, and if you find you have been at fault, then ask pardon of the Lord with humility while making a firm resolution to correct your faulty conduct."[2]

"May the ever-present grace of the Lord prevent you from being a prey to the evil one, even to the slightest extent. It is never a small matter when a soul espoused to the Son of God succumbs to the wiles of this dreadful monster, even in little things. Never let your mind become so absorbed in your work or in other matters as to make you lose the presence of God."[3]

PRAYER

Lord, teach me to acknowledge and trust in Your presence always. Amen.

96
To Your Advantage

✠

From Psalm 96: "For he is coming to judge the earth. He will judge the world with righteousness, and the peoples with his truth."[1]

I know I'll receive God's worst judgment because I'm sure to fall.

ST. PIO'S WORDS

"Oh, beloved of Jesus, if you were left to yourself, you would always be falling and never remain on your feet. Humble yourself, then, at the delightful thought that you are in the divine arms of Jesus, the best of fathers, like a little infant in its mother's arms. Sleep peacefully with the certainty that you are being guided towards the destination which will be to your greatest advantage."[2]

"Always keep Jesus' obedience in the Garden and on the cross before your eyes. This obedience of His was accomplished with immense struggle and without comfort, but He obeyed to the point of complaining to... His Father. And Jesus' obedience was excellent and beautiful in proportion to its painfulness. Therefore, your soul was never more acceptable to God as it is, now that you obey and serve Him in aridity and as a blind person."[3]

PRAYER

Lord, thank You that even in my "blindness" You won't let me fall. Amen.

97

Peace of Soul

＋

From Psalm 97: "The LORD loves those who hate evil."[1]

I do hate evil, but I worry that its power will overcome and defeat me.

ST. PIO'S WORDS

"... I feel more and more prepared to meet any suffering which may come, as long as it is a matter of pleasing Jesus. It is true that the evil one cannot refrain from his efforts to make me lose my peace of soul and lessen the great confidence I have in the divine Mercy. The enemy tries to do this chiefly by means of continual temptations. . . . I laugh at all this as being of no account. It sometimes worries me, though, that I am not quite sure if I have been ready to put up a fight at the enemy's very first attack. But when I examine my conscience, I realize that I would prefer to die rather than deliberately offend our dear Jesus by a single sin, however small."[2]

"Fear nothing because it is precisely Jesus who is working within you. You are not offending Him at all. Without a doubt, it is the enemy who wants to convince you to the contrary. Despise and scorn him, in the name of holy obedience."[3]

PRAYER

Lord, help me to always discern what is evil and then to reject it. Amen.

98
Your Joy

From Psalm 98: "Make a joyful noise to the LORD."[1]

If I feel no joy, how can I make a "joyful noise" to God?

ST. PIO'S WORDS

"Love has as its close relatives joy and peace. Joy is born of happiness at possessing what you love. Now, from the moment at which the soul knows God, it is naturally led to love Him. If the soul follows this natural impulse, which is caused by the Holy Spirit, it is already loving the supreme Good. This fortunate soul already possesses the beautiful virtue of love. By loving God, the soul is certain of possessing Him. [Unfortunately], when a person loves money, honors, and good health, he does not always possess what he loves, whereas he who loves God possesses Him at once. . . .

"Joy, then, is an offspring of love, but if this joy is to be true and perfect, it must be accompanied by the peace which pervades you when the good you possess is supreme and certain. Now, is not God the supreme Good which your soul loves and possesses as the result of loving Him? . . . Our divine Master assures you that no one will take your joy from you."[2]"[3]

PRAYER

Lord, help me love You, so I can make a "joyful noise" unto You. Amen.

99

Let the Holy Spirit Act in You

✠

From Psalm 99: "Holy is he!"[1]

I've tried to imitate Jesus' holiness, but I've failed. What should I do?

ST. PIO'S WORDS

"[Rely on] the Holy Spirit to fill you with His most holy gifts. May He sanctify you, guide you along the path to eternal salvation, and comfort you in your innumerable troubles."[2]

"Be watchful and never place too much trust in yourself or count excessively on your own strength. . . .[3] Place all your trust in God and don't be too eager to be set free from your present state. Let the Holy Spirit act within you. Give yourself up to all His [movements in your soul] and have no fear. He is so wise and gentle and discreet that He never brings about anything but good. How good this Holy Spirit, this Comforter, is to all, but how supremely good He is to those who seek Him."[4]

"Throw yourself confidently into the arms of the heavenly Father with childlike trust. Open wide your heart to the charisma of the Holy Spirit who is only waiting for a sign from you in order to enrich you."[5]

PRAYER

Lord, here is my poor heart, now open to You. Thy will be done. Amen.

100
Clothe Yourself in Jesus

✠

From Psalm 100: "It is he that made us, and we are his; we are his people, and the sheep of his pasture."[1]

Of all God's sheep, I need a Shepherd the most.

ST. PIO'S WORDS

"Jesus loves you and wants you totally for Himself. Therefore you have no other arms with which to carry yourself, other than His; no other breast on which to rest, except His and His Providence. Don't look anywhere else, and don't dwell on anyone except Him. Keep your will, thus simply united to Him, so that there is nothing between you and Himself.

"No longer think of friendship, your body, your soul, or your sufferings. And finally, don't think of what you are unable to do, but rather, think of what you can do and do it well, for the love of the Bridegroom . . . because you have already placed everything in God. Clothe yourself in Jesus Christ Crucified; love Him in His sufferings; say many short ejaculatory prayers while thinking of this. No longer do what you are obliged to do out of inclination, but do it because it is the will of God."[2]

PRAYER

Bridegroom, Shepherd, Crucified One, Thy will be done. Amen.

101
Lies and Deception

✠

From Psalm 101: "No one who practices deceit shall remain in my house; no one who utters lies shall continue in my presence."[1]

I do my best to obey God, so that I can live forever in His presence, but I fear I'm still not worthy.

ST. PIO'S WORDS

"I know that you adhere to obedience and directions and that you gain merit through this. And if it appears to you that you do not do this, or that you waste it, this is false, a lie; and it is a lie insinuated by the evil one, in order to torture you. Reject him with contempt, and reject everything in the name of holy obedience. Do not believe in the present unworthiness and iniquity of your heart. By all means be horrified at the thought of what you might have been and still could be, but rejoice also — as you have every right to do — thanking the mercy of the heavenly Father that you are not what you could have been, if His vigilant grace had not assisted you."[2]

"Don't fear, because all fear is truly useless and senseless. . . . Don't fear as regards your spirit because the Lord is with you and watches over you."[3]

PRAYER

Thank You that I can live a holy life by Christ's strength.[4] *Amen.*

102
Your Faithful Friend

✠

From Psalm 102: "I am like a lonely bird on the housetop."[1]

Especially when I'm troubled and suffering, I feel all alone.

ST. PIO'S WORDS

"Never say you are alone in the battles against your enemies. Never say you have nobody to whom you can open up and confide. You would do your heavenly messenger [your guardian angel] a grave wrong."[2]

"Never forget your guardian angel... who never leaves you.... May this most faithful friend save you from unfaithfulness."[3]

"If all people could only understand and appreciate the great gift which God, in His exceeding love, has given us by appointing heavenly spirits to guide us. Often call to mind your angel's presence. Fix your spiritual gaze on him. Thank him. . . . He is so considerate and sensitive. Respect him. You must always be afraid to offend the purity of his gaze."[4]

"May the Virgin Mother be the very one who obtains for you the strength and courage to fight valiantly. May your good angel be your breastplate to ward off the blows that the enemies of your salvation aim at you."[5]

PRAYER

Lord, thank You for my good angel who will always guard me. Amen.

103
God's Compassionate Hand

✛

From Psalm 103: "He does not deal with us according to our sins, nor repay us according to our iniquities."[1]

But I deserve hell.

ST. PIO'S WORDS

"[The person] who is crushed by the sight of the wounds produced by his own failings, and who drags himself along, face downward, in the dust, this person triumphs over God's justice. The person who humbles himself, weeps, sighs, and prays . . . obliges God to show him mercy.[2]"[3]

"Take heart, even when you feel oppressed by the great number and ugliness of your offences. Then, more than ever, you should come to the feet of Jesus Christ, who is fighting and enduring agony for you in the Garden. Humble yourself, weep, and plead with Him and like Him [to the heavenly Father]. Ask with loud cries for God's mercy, for His forgiveness of your faults, and for help to walk all the time in His sight. Do this and have no doubt that this merciful God will stretch out a compassionate hand, as He has always done, to lift you out of your spiritual desolation."[4]

PRAYER

Lord, have mercy on me and help me to walk always in Your sight. Amen.

104
God of Light

⊞

From Psalm 104: "O LORD my God, you are very great. You are...
wrapped in light as with a garment"[1]

But instead of with light, my soul is wrapped in darkness.

ST. PIO'S WORDS

"The shadows which have fallen on your soul do not come from
the Father of Light, but from the tempter who wants to torment
you."[2]

"You have every reason to be frightened when you measure the
trial by your own strength, but the knowledge that Jesus never
leaves you should bring you the greatest consolation. God tells us
that He is with those who are afflicted and in distress. . . .[3] Be comforted, then, by the delightful thought that after such pitch darkness the beautiful noonday sun will shine. In this light you will
contemplate our heavenly Spouse with a clear, transparent gaze.
Do not be inclined to believe that for you there is no salvation.
Cast this thought far from you, for it comes from our common
enemy. Arm yourself with the beautiful virtue of trust in the Lord
and take heed of the assurances which God gives you through
me."[4]

PRAYER

Lord of Light, I will trust You even in the darkness. Amen.

105

Is God Not Faithful?

✠

From Psalm 105: "He is mindful of his covenant forever."[1]

But when life's storms toss me around, how can I trust God to keep His covenant, His promises?

ST. PIO'S WORDS

"Trust in the Lord . . . always place your confidence in Jesus, and He will know how to comfort your soul, even when it is tossed about in a stormy sea. Never be afraid of the enemy's enticements, for no matter how strong they may be, they will never avail to sweep you into the enemy's nets, as long as you remain faithful to the Lord and on your guard, while you build up your strength by prayer and holy humility. God has promised that He opposes the proud but gives grace to the humble;[2] that those who watch and pray will not enter into temptation.[3]

"What are you afraid of, then? Is our God not faithful to His promises?"[4]

"For pity's sake, flee from these useless fears the moment they rise up in you. Never despair of the divine assistance."[5]

PRAYER

Lord God, help me to always "watch and pray" and to trust in Your divine assistance. Amen.

106

Praise for Divine Assistance

✠

From Psalm 106: "Blessed be the LORD, the God of Israel. . . ."[1]

Instead of always petitioning God, I should praise Him.

ST. PIO'S WORDS

"I praise and bless God for His continual assistance in your regard and for the way He helps you to bear your trials without wavering. All the same, in you there is some anxiety and longing which hinder the full effect of your patience. By your patience you will possess your soul,[2] Jesus tells us. It is therefore through patience that you will possess your soul. To the extent to which your patience is perfect, will be the extent to which your possession of your soul will be entire, perfect, and certain. The less your patience is mixed with longings and anxiety, the more perfect is your patience.

"You are suffering because you [feel as if your soul is in exile] . . . but remember this, that the children of Israel remained forty years in the desert before taking possession of the promised land. . . . Courage then, and carry on peacefully. Jesus will invariably help you."[3]

PRAYER

Lord Jesus, please help me to patiently trust in You and to always praise and thank You. Amen.

107
May This Thought Console You

✠

From Psalm 107: "Then they cried to the LORD in their trouble, and he brought them out from their distress."[1]

Every day, old and new conflicts manage to upset me.

ST. PIO'S WORDS

"... I experience a deep spiritual joy in seeing how much God loves you. The storm that is raging around you and upsetting you is a sure sign of this love. This is not just a personal conviction of mine, but an argument from Scripture which tells us that combat is proof of the soul's union with God and an indication of God's presence deep down in the soul. 'I will be with them in trouble.'[2] Hence the Apostle James exhorts people to rejoice when they are tormented by various calamities and numerous contradictions.[3] The reason is that the crown is won in combat, and the better the soul fights, the more the palms [eternal glory] are multiplied. If you realize that every victory you obtain has a corresponding degree of eternal glory, how can you fail to rejoice when you find yourself obliged to face many trials in the course of your life? May this thought console you."[4]

PRAYER

Teach me to rejoice when facing trouble and rest in You. Amen.

108
Tender Mother

✠

From Psalm 108: "With God we shall do valiantly; it is he who will tread down our foes."[1]

Still, I fear the enemy, and I wonder how God can save me.

ST. PIO'S WORDS

"If you do not intend to surrender, have no illusion about the enemy who is exceedingly strong. In the light infused by God, your soul understands the great danger to which it is exposed if it is not continually on its guard. The idea of losing all by a possible fall makes your poor soul tremble. . . .

"The strength of the evil one who fights against you is terrible, but may God be praised, for He has placed the cause of your salvation and the ultimate victory in the hands of your heavenly Mother. Protected and guided by so tender a Mother, continue to fight as long as God wills, full of confidence . . . and certain that you will never succumb.

"How far away is the hope of victory, viewed from this land of exile! How close and certain it is, on the other hand, when viewed from God's house, beneath the protection of this most holy Mother."[2]

PRAYER

Lord, thank You for placing me in the care of Your tender Mother. Amen.

109
Your Miserable and Poor Heart

✠

From Psalm 109: "For I am poor and needy, and my heart is pierced."[1]

When fear and pain pierce my heart, what should I do?

ST. PIO'S WORDS

"What happiness it would be if one day, returning home from Mass, you were to find your miserable, poor heart outside your breast, and in its place, the precious Heart of our God! But since you must not desire such great and extraordinary things, I at least desire that your heart live only under obedience and by the commandments of the Heart of this Lord.

"Therefore... imitate St. Catherine in a fruitful manner in this. In this way, you will be sweet, humble, and charitable because the Heart of Jesus has no law more lovable than that of sweetness, humility, and charity.

"... In Arabia, when shepherds hear thunder and see the air filled with lightning, they retire with their flocks under the laurel bushes.... When you see that persecutions and contradictions are forewarning you of some great displeasure, retire with confidence under the cross... because all will work out to your benefit because you love God."[2]

PRAYER

Lord, if troubles pierce my heart, I'll take refuge under the cross. Amen.

110
His Powerful Hand

✞

From Psalm 110: "Sit at my right hand until I make your enemies your footstool."[1]

Until God defeats all of Christ's enemies — and mine — what should I do?

ST. PIO'S WORDS

"Be steadfast and firm in your faith, and be on the alert, for in this way you will avoid the enemy's evil snares. This is the warning given by the Apostle Peter. . . .[2] Yes, renew your faith in the truths of Christian doctrine, especially during times of conflict. And renew your faith in the promise of eternal life which Jesus makes to those who fight energetically and courageously. You should be encouraged and comforted by the knowledge that you are not alone in your sufferings, for all the followers of Jesus the Nazarene suffer in the same manner. . . .

"Humble yourself beneath His powerful hand; cheerfully accept the trials to which the mercy of our Father subjects you, so that He may raise you up at the time of His visitation. . . . Love God, be pleasing to Him, and pay no attention to the rest, knowing God will always take care of you."[3]

PRAYER

Thank You for the comfort of knowing I'm not alone in suffering. Amen.

III
With This Safe Guide

✠

From Psalm 111: "The fear of the LORD is the beginning of wisdom."[1]

I do fear God, but I also worry I'm always offending Him.

ST. PIO'S WORDS

"As regards your fear of offending God and of not knowing how to please Him, I beseech you to calm your anxiety. Believe the assurances of authority which tell you, on behalf of God, that however you act, as long as you do not clearly see your actions to be contrary to the law of God and the established authorities, Jesus is always pleased with you, when your actions are directed for the glory of God.

"With this safe guide, you must act without questioning; you must go forward without heeding the voice of your fears. Note that I say 'heed,' that is to 'pay attention and agree with them.' I don't say you are not to *hear* them, because you can't help this, but don't worry about them. Carry on with your activities, just as you do when you ignore the barks of a little dog. . . . Certainly you *hear* those tiresome barks, but you ignore them."[2]

PRAYER

Lord, help me to please You and to ignore my unreasonable fears. Amen.

112
Light and Darkness

✠

From Psalm 112: "The desire of the wicked comes to nothing."[1]

The wickedness in this world makes me wonder if I'm wicked too.

ST. PIO'S WORDS

"You do not do wrong without being aware of it. If you acted badly, you should see it quite clearly. How can a person be condemned if he is not conscious of his error? Moreover, light and darkness cannot be present at the same time. Now, if you had done wrong, you would know it, but with your eyes open, can you still maintain that you did wrong? The solution lies with you. . . . You are with Jesus, and Jesus is closely united with you. Listen to His voice. Put away the fears you have. . . . God is with you, and not a hair of your head will be touched.[2]

" . . . I ask you to place great importance on reading holy books as much as you can. This spiritual reading is as necessary to you as the air you breathe. Read, read a great deal, and never fail to add a fervent and humble prayer to your good reading."[3]

PRAYER

Lord, I promise to read only holy books that lead me into Your Light and away from the darkness of the wicked. Amen.

113

Such a Loving Spouse

✠

From Psalm 113: "Who is like the LORD our God, who is seated on high, who looks far down on the heavens and the earth?"[1]

From His throne in heaven, why would God pay attention to me?

ST. PIO'S WORDS

"The Lord is with you, always ready to welcome what you confide to Him in secret."[2]

"I urge you to have ever-greater confidence in God, for it is written that those who trust in Him will never be forsaken....[3] In the midst of the trials which afflict you, place all your confidence in our supreme Good, in the knowledge that He takes more care of us than a mother takes of her child.

"Don't allow sadness to dwell in your soul, for sadness prevents the Holy Spirit from acting freely. If you insist on being sad, then let it be a holy sadness at the sight of the evil that is spreading in society nowadays. Many poor souls are every day deserting God, our supreme Good! . . .

"The Lord is with you. . . . What a great consolation it is to know that you always have access to such a dear Friend, to such a loving Spouse!"[4]

PRAYER

Lord, thank You for being my Friend, my Spouse, and my Savior. Amen.

114
You Are Not Wicked

✠

From Psalm 114: "Tremble, O earth, at the presence of the LORD."[1]

I will never be good enough to be in God's presence.

ST. PIO'S WORDS

"Calm your anxiety because the grace that renders your soul acceptable to God dwells in your heart. Your soul . . . is in the 'hall' of the Lord. And whenever you try to convince yourself of this, you fear the contrary because the human heart doesn't want to believe what is good for it. . . .

"Don't let the assaults of the enemy frighten you, and do not worry about the future. He who defended you will continue to do so. Therefore, be consoled in afflictions, and let your great sadness be in peace. . . . The light increases, and soon it is midday when the soul is dilated in the sun. But when the sun goes down, and darkness follows, you no longer remember the light, and the Lord withdraws even the memory of the consolation enjoyed, so that the shadows may be complete. Calm yourself . . . these shadows are not a punishment proportioned to your wickedness. You are not wicked, nor are you blinded by your own malice."[2]

PRAYER

Lord, thank You for Your grace that makes me acceptable to You. Amen.

115
He Is Within You

✠

From Psalm 115: "You who fear the LORD, trust in the LORD!"[1]

It's easy for me to fear, but it's hard for me to trust.

ST. PIO'S WORDS

"Do not anticipate the problems of this life with apprehension, but rather with a perfect hope that God, to whom you belong, will free you from them accordingly. He has defended you up to now. Simply hold on tightly to the hand of His divine Providence, and He will help you in all events, and when you are unable to walk, He will lead you, so don't worry. Do not fear when you belong to this God who strongly assures you, 'We know that all things work together for good for those who love God.'[2] Don't think about tomorrow's events because the same heavenly Father who takes care of you today will do the same tomorrow and forever. . . .

"Live tranquilly; remove from your imagination that which upsets you, and often say to the Lord, 'Oh God, you are my God, and I will trust in You. You will assist me and be my refuge, and I will fear nothing.' Not only are you *with* Him, but you are *in* Him, and He is within you."[3]

PRAYER

Lord, with You as my refuge, I truly have nothing to fear. Amen.

116

This Great Mercy

✠

From Psalm 116: "I love the LORD, because he has heard my voice."[1]

I do love God with all my heart, but how can He love me, a sinner?

ST. PIO'S WORDS

"Since the Lord is able to obtain good even from evil, for whom will He do this if not for those who have given themselves to Him without reservation? Even sin itself, which God keeps far from you by His goodness, is used for the good of those who serve Him, by His Providence.

"If the holy King David had never sinned, he would never have acquired a profound humility; nor would Mary Magdalene have ardently loved Jesus if He had not forgiven her for her many sins and if she had not committed them.

"Consider the work of this great mercy. It converts your sins into good, and with the venom of them makes a medicine which is healthy for your soul. Therefore, what will He not do with your afflictions, with the troubles and persecutions which upset you? If you suffer for your afflictions, if you love God with all your heart... everything will be converted to good."[2]

PRAYER

Thank You for Your mercy that can convert even me *into a saint. Amen.*

117
Guided by His Love

✠

From Psalm 117: "For great is his steadfast love toward us, and the faithfulness of the LORD endures forever."[1]

If God loves me, will He calm my anxieties?

ST. PIO'S WORDS

"I urge you in the charity of Christ to make sure you calm your anxiety by drinking at the fountain of divine Love, which you must do by faith and trust, by humility and submission to God's will. Saint Therese of the Child Jesus said she was just a little soul who chose neither to live nor to die. She told Jesus to do what He wanted with her. Here is the example of a soul completely stripped of self and filled with God! This is precisely what you also must strive to become, with divine assistance.

"Don't be distrustful in this respect, for Jesus is in your soul, and if you show yourself docile to His actions, you will certainly [be filled with God]. I understand, however, that the anxiety of a soul on fire for its divine Lover often becomes uncontrollable, but don't be scared by this. Just give free reign to this longing for Jesus and let yourself be guided by His Love."[2]

PRAYER

Lord, strip me of myself and fill me with You. Amen.

118
The Cornerstone

✠

From Psalm 118: "The stone [Jesus] that the builders rejected has become the chief cornerstone."[1]

People still *reject Jesus, especially in the Holy Eucharist.*

ST. PIO'S WORDS

"There is a prayer which you must never neglect: See how much scorn and sacrilege is committed by people towards the most-holy Humanity of God's Son in the Sacrament of Love. It is up to us, because we have been chosen beforehand by the Lord's goodness to be members of His Church. . . . It is up to us to defend the honor of this meek Lamb who is always concerned when the case of souls is in question, but always silent where His own case is concerned.

"Offer up your entire life, all your actions and desires in reparation for the offences which ungrateful people do to Him. But your thoughts must be raised higher still, to the Father who alone can and must give everything to glorify His most-holy Son. You must knock at this divine Father's Heart with confidence and pray that He will defend Jesus in the Blessed Sacrament."[2]

PRAYER

Father, thank You for Christ in the Eucharist. Please defend Him. Amen.

119
By Your Endurance

✠

From Psalm 119: "I run the way of your commandments."[1]

But during times when I feel no enthusiasm or eagerness in serving and obeying God, I fear I might be offending Him.

ST. PIO'S WORDS

"When the Lord tests you with aridity, you often lose your tranquility and submit reluctantly to the test. You become a prey to a thousand apprehensions, while there is no need for this, for even during this time of testing you possess true devotion to and love of God.

"If you were to question yourself, you would recognize that, in this state, you also have an inclination and readiness to do what you know pleases God. Isn't this evidence sufficient to convince you that your soul is extremely attached to God and that God does not cast it off?

"Can you doubt that you possess the virtues of charity and piety? Haven't you sufficient reason to cry out with King David, 'I run the way of your commandments'[2]? Set charity and piety in order, and then it will be possible to say of you also: 'By your endurance you will gain your soul'[3]"[4]

PRAYER

Lord, even when I feel no love or devotion, I'll still follow You. Amen.

120
Continual Contentment

✠

From Psalm 120: "Too long have I had my dwelling among those who hate peace."[1]

I'm ashamed that I have allowed the enemy of peace to upset me.

ST. PIO'S WORDS

"The enemy of your salvation knows that peace of heart is a sure sign of the divine assistance, and so the enemy misses no opportunity to make you lose this peace. You must always be on your guard. . . . Jesus will help you."[2]

"You will never advance in the virtue [of simplicity] if you do not strive to live in holy and unchangeable peace. Jesus' yoke is easy and His burden light, so you should not allow the enemy to creep into your heart and rob you of this peace.

"Peace is simplicity of heart, serenity of mind, tranquility of soul, and the bond of love. Peace means order and harmony in your whole being; it means continual contentment springing from the knowledge of a good conscience; it is the holy joy of a heart in which God reigns. Peace is the way to perfection; indeed, in peace is perfection to be found."[3]

PRAYER

Lord, let Your peace reign in my heart and lead me to perfection. Amen.

121
Continual Victory

✠

From Psalm 121: "The LORD will keep you from all evil; he will keep your life."[1]

Maybe I'm too miserable of a creature for God to protect.

ST. PIO'S WORDS

"May God be blessed for all the great mercy He shows to me! Miserable creature that I am and deserving every punishment for my scanty faithfulness to God, I feel confused. Still, I don't feel disheartened, due to the grace our good Jesus bestows on me. . . .

"When will . . . Jesus consume me entirely by His holy love? When can I be utterly consumed by the divine fire? When can I be so closely united to Him that I can sing a completely new song, the canticle of victory? When will there be an end to this interior combat between evil and my poor soul, which wants to belong entirely to its heavenly Spouse?

"My weakness makes me tremble and to break out in cold perspiration. . . . But from God alone, through Jesus Christ, I hope for the grace to obtain the victory continually, and never to be defeated."[2]

PRAYER

Lord, in spite of my failings, please always protect me from defeat. Amen.

122
House of God

From Psalm 122: "I was glad when they said to me, 'Let us go to the house of the LORD!'"[1]

When in church, how should I act, in order to please God?

ST. PIO'S WORDS

"In order to avoid irreverence in the house of God, in church... enter in silence and with great respect, considering yourself unworthy to appear before the Lord's Majesty.... Your soul is the temple of God and, as such, you must keep it pure and spotless before God and His angels. Blush for having allowed the evil one and... His enticements of the world, his pomp, and his tempting of the flesh to keep your heart from being pure and your body chaste; for having allowed your enemies to enter your heart, thus desecrating the temple of God, which you became through holy baptism. Take holy water, make the sign of the cross carefully, and when you are before God in the Blessed Sacrament, genuflect. [Once you are in your pew], confide all your needs to Him, along with those of others.... Give Him free rein of your heart and total freedom to work in you as He thinks best."[2]

PRAYER

Lord, even when I'm not in church, work in me as You will. Amen.

123
Lord, I Need Patience

✠

From Psalm 123: "As the eyes of servants look to the hand of their master... so our eyes look to the LORD our God."[1]

When trouble strikes, I wish I'd look to God rather than at my sufferings.

ST. PIO'S WORDS

"Let your entire life be spent in resignation, prayer, work, humility, and in rendering thanks to the good God. If you happen to notice a feeling of impatience arising, immediately have recourse to prayer. Consider that you are always in the presence of God, to whom you have to give an account for your every action, both good and bad. Above all, turn your thoughts to the annihilation which the Son of God suffered for love of you. I want the thought of the suffering and humiliation of Jesus to be the usual subject of your meditation. If you practice this, as I am sure you will, in a short time you will experience its wholesome fruits. Such meditation will act as a shield to defend you from impatience when the most-sweet Jesus sends you suffering, places you in a state of desolation, or wishes to make you a subject of contradiction."[2]

PRAYER

Now, whenever I suffer, I'll meditate on You, my Crucified Lord. Amen.

124
Divine Benevolence

☩

From Psalm 124: If it had not been the LORD who was on our side . . . then over us would have gone the raging waters."[1]

Why would God help me, a weak sinner?

ST. PIO'S WORDS

"At the sight of all the help which Jesus offers me with such liberality, I can't contain my gratitude. In the midst of the extreme desolation in which the Lord has placed me, I feel gratitude rise up like a giant in my heart. But as a grace, this is a thousand miles from my spirit, or rather, admitting that it is a grace for me, I do not believe it is for my good, for I see clearly that my soul is unworthy of God's light which enlightens every person. . . .

"I am resigned to everything and feel prepared for anything. May the Lord do with me whatever is most pleasing to Him. . . . Considering myself unworthy of the divine gaze, and seeing the divine benevolence towards me, my heart cannot contain itself. . . . May He accept the homage of my gratitude. May He be blessed, honored, and glorified a thousand times, and may He be praised in heaven and on earth, as He deserves."[2]

PRAYER

Merciful Lord, do with me as You please, and accept my gratitude. Amen.

125
The Lord Is with You

✢

From Psalm 125: "As the mountains surround Jerusalem, so the LORD surrounds his people."[1]

If God surrounds me, why does worry haunt me?

ST. PIO'S WORDS

"Do not worry because that would be harmful to your soul. The intrusion of worry, to a greater or lesser degree, diminishes charity of heart and trust in God. This must not be considered a small matter because it prevents the Holy Spirit from acting freely in your heart.

"Leave all concerns to the most-sweet Spouse of souls; lay your head on the breast of this most-tender Spouse, as a beloved disciple, and do not fear the uproar of the mob [yelling for the arrest of Jesus in the Garden], for the heavenly Master will not allow a hair of your head to be touched, just as He did not allow His disciples to be harmed in the Garden of Gethsemane. Then, in the midst of the disrespectful crowd, you will ascend, unobserved, with your King to the summit of Calvary. Prostrate yourself before the Lord with humility of heart. Have no fear, for the Lord is with you."[2]

PRAYER

Lord, I leave my worries behind and humbly trust in You. Amen.

126
Praise the Divine Prisoner

✠

From Psalm 126: "The LORD has done great things for us."[1]

God's goodness to me, a sinner, sometimes overwhelms me, rendering me speechless and almost in tears.

ST. PIO'S WORDS

"When Mass was over, I remained with Jesus in thanksgiving. Sweet was the conversation with paradise that morning! Although I want to tell you all about it, I cannot. There were things which cannot be translated into human language without losing their deep, heavenly meaning. The Heart of Jesus and my own . . . were fused. No longer were we two hearts beating, but only one. My heart had disappeared, just as a drop of water is lost in the ocean. Jesus was its paradise, its King. My joy was so intense and deep, I could bear no more, and tears of happiness poured down my cheeks.

"Yes, people cannot understand that when paradise is poured into a heart, this . . . weak and mortal heart cannot bear it without weeping. I repeat, it was the joy that filled my heart which caused me to weep for so long. This visit, believe me, restored me completely. Praise be to the divine Prisoner!"[2]

PRAYER

Thank You for continually blessing me, although I am unworthy. Amen.

127
Strength in God Alone

✠

From Psalm 127: "Unless the LORD guards the city, the guard keeps watch in vain."[1]

When I try to fight temptations on my own, I fall.

ST. PIO'S WORDS

"Valiantly fight temptations, along with strong souls, and fight along with the supreme Chief [God]. When you fall, do not stay there prostrated in body and spirit. Humble yourself greatly, but without being discouraged. Wash your imperfections and your falls with sincere tears of contrition, without lacking trust in divine goodness, which will always be greater than your ingratitude. Propose to make amends without being presumptuous, but your strength must be in God alone. Finally, confess sincerely that if God were not your breastplate and shield, you would be pierced with every kind of sin. And it is for this reason that you must always keep yourself in the grace of God, with perseverance in carrying out your spiritual exercises. Let this be your principal concern.

". . . I leave you in the Heart of Jesus. In Him, let us find each other."[2]

PRAYER

Lord, forgive me for thinking I can fight temptation without You. Amen.

128

Fire of Love

✠

From Psalm 128: "You shall be happy, and it shall go well with you."[1]

What should I do to obtain that holy happiness?

ST. PIO'S WORDS

"How happy is the interior kingdom, when holy love reigns there! How blessed are the faculties of the soul when they obey so wise a King! Under obedience to Him and in His realm, He doesn't permit serious sins to dwell. . . . It is true that He often allows sin to arrive at His frontiers, so that in the combat, the virtues may be practiced and strengthened. It is equally true that He permits the master spies — venial sins and imperfections — to circulate freely in His kingdom, but this is merely to show you that, without Him, you would be a prey for your enemies.

"Humble yourself. . . . You must keep alight in your heart the fire of love and never lose courage. If listlessness or spiritual weakness overtakes you, hasten to the foot of the cross . . . and you will undoubtedly be invigorated.

"May the grace of Jesus be always with you!"[2]

PRAYER

Lord, You are my happiness. Keep Your love burning within me. Amen.

129
Not a Hair of Your Head

✠

From Psalm 129: "Often have they attacked me from my youth, yet they have not prevailed against me."[1]

When all kinds of troubles, trials, and suffering attack, will God help me?

ST. PIO'S WORDS

"My soul in the state [of suffering] seems to glimpse a concealed hand, which can be none other than the hand of God. At the apex of my spirit, I feel... the divine Master's most-beautiful assurance that not a hair of my head will perish without the permission of our heavenly Father,[2] that He watches over my soul with fatherly love, and that when He tests it by similar desolation, He invariably does so out of love and for my soul's perfection.

"Hence, the bitterness of the trial is sweetened by the balm of God's goodness and mercy. Praise be to God who can so marvelously alternate joy and tears, so as to lead the soul by unknown paths to the attainment of perfection, a flower which the merciful God causes to bloom amid the thorns of suffering, watered by the tears of the soul that suffers patiently, that humbly conforms to the divine will and prays with warmth and fervor."[3]

PRAYER

Thank You for the Love that never allows bitter trials to defeat me. Amen.

130
Most-Delicious Fruit

✠

From Psalm 130: "Out of the depths I cry to you, O LORD."[1]

When my weaknesses and wretchedness glare at me, my soul feels pain, sadness, and distress.

ST. PIO'S WORDS

"Tell me, is it the sun or is it darkness that lights up and discloses things? I leave it to you to draw the true conclusion. God alone is His grace, God alone is the supreme Sun, and all others are nothing, or if they are anything, it is due to Him alone. God alone, I say, can enlighten you with His grace and show you what you are. And the more fully you know your own wretchedness and unworthiness in God's sight, the more remarkable is the grace that enlightens you and reveals to you what you are.

"I understand that the discovery of your own wretchedness under the action of this divine Sun saddens and distresses you at first. It is a source of pain and of terror for the soul. . . . But console yourself in our most-sweet Lord, for when this divine Sun warms your soul with its burning rays, it will cause new plants to spring up, which will yield most-delicious fruit."[2]

PRAYER

Lord, warm my soul and cause "new plants," virtues, to grow. Amen.

131
Like a Child

✛

From Psalm 131: "O Lord . . . I do not occupy myself with things too great and too marvelous for me. But I have calmed and quieted my soul, like a weaned child with its mother."[1]

Often I complicate my life by trying to do things too difficult for me.

ST. PIO'S WORDS

"Jesus likes to give Himself to simple souls. You must make an effort to acquire this beautiful virtue of simplicity and to hold it in great esteem. Jesus said, 'Truly I tell you, unless you change and become like children, you will never enter the kingdom of heaven.'[2] But before He taught us this by His words, He had already put it into practice. He became a child and gave us the example of that simplicity He was to teach us later by His words. Empty your heart. . . . Try to keep your thoughts pure, your ideas upright and honest, and your intentions holy.

"Also, endeavor to have a will that seeks nothing but God and His glory. If you make every effort to advance in this beautiful virtue, He who teaches it will enrich you continually with new light and new heavenly favors."[3]

PRAYER

Lord, teach me to embrace simplicity and "become like a child." Amen.

132
God Resides in Your Soul

✠

From Psalm 132: "For the LORD has chosen Zion [your heart]; he has desired it for his habitation: 'This is my resting place forever; here I will reside, for I have desired it.'"[1]

If God has chosen to dwell in me, why do I commit faults and feel pain?

ST. PIO'S WORDS

"Every slightest fault I commit is like a sword of sorrow piercing my heart. At certain moments I am led to exclaim with the apostle . . . 'I have been crucified with Christ; and it is no longer I who live, but it is Christ who lives in me.'[2]"[3]

"I am an instrument in divine hands; an instrument which only succeeds in serving some purpose when it is handled by the divine Craftsman. Left to my own devices, I can do nothing but sin, and sin again. . . .

"Place all your cares in God alone, as He has supreme care of you, and His vigilant grace will see that you always triumph over all the evil deceit of the enemy."[4]

"May your heart always be the temple of Jesus!"[5]

PRAYER

Lord, I am Yours. Take charge of my heart, Your "resting place." Amen.

133
Your Heavenly Home

+

From Psalm 133: "There [heaven] the LORD ordained his blessing, life forevermore."[1]

Life seems so long and so difficult; will I ever reach heaven?

ST. PIO'S WORDS

"Ask the Holy Spirit, the Comforter, to enlighten you with regard to His great truths. . . . First, ask Him to make you aware of the excellence of your Christian calling. Consider the fact that you were chosen, elected from innumerable others. And know that, without any merit on your part, this election was decided by God from all eternity, before the foundation of the world,[2] for the sole reason that you might be His eternally in heaven. This is such a great and enchanting mystery, that your soul, even though it understands little of all this, cannot but melt away with love.

"Second, pray that the Spirit may enlighten you about the immensity of the eternal inheritance which has been reserved for you by the goodness of the heavenly Father. May contemplating this mystery turn your heart away from earthly goods and make you eager to reach your heavenly home."[3]

PRAYER

Contemplating Your endless love of me makes me long for heaven. Amen.

134
Your Guide, Your Ship, Your Port

✠

From Psalm 134: "Lift up your hands to the holy place, and bless the LORD."[1]

How can I bless God when my pain hides Him from me?

ST. PIO'S WORDS

"What is this painful searching for God which occupies your heart? It is the effect of love which draws you and love which impels you. Then why does love take flight? Recall that Mary turned to stone in the presence of her crucified Son, but she was not abandoned. When, indeed, was her love stronger than at that moment when she suffered and could not even weep?

"Console yourself then.... During times of tribulation, defend yourself as best you can, and when you don't succeed, be resigned to see night falling without becoming frightened.... Do not let anything disturb you. It is still night, but day is approaching, and it will not delay in coming. Meanwhile, put into practice the saying of David, 'Lift up your hands to the holy place, and bless the LORD!'[2] Yes, bless Him with all your heart, and bless Him always, and pray that He may be your guide, your ship, and your port."[3]

PRAYER

While I await Your light to dispel the darkness, I will bless You! Amen.

135

That Beautiful Day Is Coming

✠

From Psalm 135: "For I know that the LORD is great."[1]

Yes, the Lord is great, but I worry I'll never reach heaven where I can forever fully appreciate and praise His greatness, His eternal presence.

ST. PIO'S WORDS

"Courage!... That beautiful day is already on its way, and happy are those who will be able to shout with joy, 'This is the LORD's doing.'[2] All of us will join in singing the eternal song of praise to God, for this day will appear wonderful to our eyes,[3] for the triumph of divine justice over iniquity.

"This beautiful day which is coming cannot be the work of anyone but God, and God will make it to be for the resurrection of many and the triumph of His glory. Thanks be to God!... Don't worry about your spiritual state. Jesus is with you, protecting you because He loves you. The present trial will increase grace in your soul and will be rewarded by the eternal banquet, always granted that, with God's help, you do not fail to repress every feeling which leads you to set yourself up as more than you are."[4]

PRAYER

Lord, keep me grace-filled, so I can attend Your eternal banquet. Amen.

136
A Glimmer of Light

✠

From Psalm 136: "O give thanks to the LORD, for he is good, for his steadfast love endures forever."[1]

During my tribulations, God's love radiates only a glimmer of light into my soul. I hope that small glimmer is always enough to protect me.

ST. PIO'S WORDS

"You say that while the Lord is testing you, by His crosses and sufferings, He always leaves in your heart a glimmer of light by which you continue to have great trust in Him and to see His immense goodness."[2]

" . . . Be at peace and confide in the Lord's goodness because you are very pleasing to Him. . . . Be careful and always keep a vigilant watch over yourself, especially as regards the vice of [pride in your accomplishments or qualities], which is the woodworm, the consuming moth of devout souls."[3]

"Bless the Lord, for He is good, for His mercy endures forever.[4] May Jesus . . . enable you to walk along the path that leads to Him. May the Mother of Jesus and your Mother always look on your soul with a smile."[5]

PRAYER

Lord, You are good and merciful. May Your Mother's smile and Your light and love keep me on the path to You. Amen.

137
Why Are You Sorrowful?

✠

From Psalm 137: "How could we sing the LORD's song...?"[1]

In life's dark valleys, I can't sing happy songs to God.

ST. PIO'S WORDS

"When will that happy day dawn when your soul, which is at present subjected to suffering by the divine Lord, be placed in the immense sea of eternal Truth, where it will no longer be free to offend the divine Lover ... because all its sufferings will be over?...When will there be an end to all your fears, to all your yearnings?

"When will the day dawn when you will sing happy hymns to the Lord and your heart will no longer be tormented by remorse for its inability to love as much as it feels the need to love?...Your soul will not enter into its eternal rest until it is lost forever in that vast ocean of goodness where it will know what God knows, love what He loves, and only enjoy what He enjoys. Happy should be your soul because its name is written in the book of eternal life!... Why then are you so sorrowful...? Rise up from your dejection and send up a hymn of praise ... to your Savior and Lord."[2]

PRAYER

Immerse me in Your goodness, and I'll sing that hymn of praise. Amen.

138
Fire of His Love

✠

From Psalm 138: "The LORD will fulfill his purpose for me; your steadfast love, O LORD, endures forever."[1]

But I know I've done nothing to deserve God's love.

ST. PIO'S WORDS

"My heart has found at last a Lover so attached to me that I am incapable of hurting Him anymore. You already know this Lover. He is the one who is never angry with those who offend Him. My heart keeps within itself an infinite number of His mercies. It knows that it doesn't have anything of value with which to glorify itself before Him. He loves me. . . .

"Whenever I ask Him what I have done to deserve such consolations, He smiles and says that nothing is refused to such an intercessor. In return, He asks me for nothing but love, but do I not, perhaps, owe Him this in gratitude? If I could only make Him happy just as He makes me happy! He is so much in love with my heart that He makes me burn with His divine fire, with the fire of His love. . . . This fire pervades my whole being. If Jesus makes us so happy on earth, what will heaven be like?"[2]

PRAYER

Lord, fill me with Your love, so that I can love You as You will. Amen.

139
God's Hand Will Sustain You

✠

From Psalm 139: "Your hand shall lead me."[1]

What if I lose my courage and let go of God's hand?

ST. PIO'S WORDS

"Your courage, which God granted you, is irremovable and constantly determined. Therefore, live tranquilly. Do not be anxious. . . . You must never fail to approach the holy banquet of the divine Lamb, as nothing will better gather your spirit than its King, nothing will warm it so much as its Sun, and nothing will dissolve it as sweetly as His balm. There is no remedy more powerful than this. . . .

"Live humbly . . . and in love with your heavenly Spouse. Do not be upset by infirmities and weaknesses. . . . Place yourself at the sweet mercy of He who sustains those who fall without intending to do so. [He sustains them] so they do not suffer harm. He picks them up so sweetly, they do not realize they have fallen because the hand of God sustains them. Nor do they realize they have been picked up, because God did so, so quickly, that they did not even know it."[2]

PRAYER

Lord, I kneel before Your sweet mercy; I praise and thank You. Amen.

140
Jesus With Me

✠

From Psalm 140: "Deliver me, O LORD, from evildoers; protect me from those who are violent, who plan evil things."[1]

My enemies want nothing but the worst for me.

ST. PIO'S WORDS

"The evil one continues to make war on me and, unfortunately, shows no sign of admitting defeat. In the first days during which I was put to the test, I was weak and became almost melancholy, but then, by degrees, this melancholy feeling passed, and I began to feel somewhat relieved. Later, when I prayed at the feet of Jesus, I seemed to feel no trace of the burden entailed in trying to overcome myself when tempted."[2]

"The evil one continues to make war on me and, up to the present, has shown no sign of admitting defeat. He wants me to be lost at all costs. He presents to my mind the painful picture of my life and, worse still, tries to lead me to thoughts of despair."[3]

". . . But I have Jesus with me, and what should I fear?"[4]

PRAYER

Lord, no matter what evils come my way, Your presence will protect me. Therefore, I shall not fear. Amen.

141
Benevolent Toward All

✠

From Psalm 141: "Set a guard over my mouth, O LORD; keep watch over the door of my lips."[1]

I try hard not to say unkind words, but sometimes I fail.

ST. PIO'S WORDS

"Nothing more clearly represents the good or bad qualities of your soul than the greater or lesser regulation of your exterior, as when you appear more or less modest. Be modest in speech, modest in laughter. . . . All this must be practiced, not out of vanity, in order to display yourself, nor out of hypocrisy, in order to appear good in the eyes of others, but rather, for the internal virtue of modesty. . . .

Therefore, be . . . careful with your words, prudent in your resolutions. Always be sparing in your speech . . . modest in your conversation. Don't be disgusting to anybody, but be benevolent toward all. . . . Let no daring word escape your lips . . . never use an ill-tempered tone of voice."[2]

"May Jesus continue to possess your heart; may He be pleased with you and make you holy!"[3]

PRAYER

Lord, by Your grace I know I can be more careful in speech. Amen.

142

He Disperses the Clouds

✠

From Psalm 142: "When my spirit is faint, you know my way. . . . Give heed to my cry, for I am brought very low."[1]

Will God lift me out of this dark valley?

ST. PIO'S WORDS

"I feel very weak, but I am not afraid, for Jesus will see my anguish and the weight that oppresses me. He has told us . . . that, 'As a father has compassion for his children, so the LORD has compassion for those who fear him'[2]

"I find happiness in my afflictions. Jesus Himself wants these, because He needs them for souls. . . . It gives me food for thought when I consider that God stoops down to beg sufferings from such a wretched creature. Is His purity not soiled by this heart of mine which harbored so much iniquity?

"There is nothing in me capable of attracting the gaze of this most-tender Jesus of ours. His goodness alone has filled my soul with many good things. . . . He follows me everywhere, revives my life poisoned by sin, and disperses the clouds which had enveloped my soul after I had sinned."[3]

PRAYER

Lord, thank You for replacing the poison in my life with Your love. Amen.

143
Guided by God's Spirit

✠

From Psalm 143: "Let your good spirit lead me on a level path."[1]

Daily bombarded by bad influences, it's hard to be good.

ST. PIO'S WORDS

"By the virtue of self-restraint, your soul can exercise control over all your senses: sight, touch, taste, smell, and hearing. By chastity, a virtue which ennobles your nature and makes it similar to that of the angels, you suppress your sensuality and detach it from forbidden pleasures. . . . Happy are you if you possess these fine virtues [along with modesty], all of them fruits of the Holy Spirit who dwells within you. [If you have these virtues], you have nothing to fear. . . .

"To allow the Holy Spirit freedom to act in you, you must mount guard over your spirit of self which, if you are not careful, seeps in even when you have disciplined your body [by practicing self-denial]. . . . St. Paul tells us, 'If we live by the Spirit, let us also be guided by the Spirit'[2]"[3]

"May the grace of the divine Spirit always possess your heart and those of all who want to belong to Jesus!"[4]

PRAYER

Lord, please fill me with your Holy Spirit and take control. Amen.

144
True Ladder to God

✠

From Psalm 144: "Stretch out your hand from on high... rescue me."[1]

While I wait for God to stretch out His hand to me, how can I climb closer to Him?

ST. PIO'S WORDS

"Take heart; look at the divine Master who prayed in the Garden, and you will discover the true ladder which unites the earth to heaven. You will discover that humility, contrition, and prayer make the distance between you and God disappear. They act in such a way that God descends to you, and you ascend to God, so that you end up understanding, loving, and possessing one another.... Always practice this great secret which Jesus taught us through His words and actions.

"Always keep in mind that in a person's struggle with other people, he fears his enemy and is injured... there are winners and losers. Whereas, where the person's struggle with God is concerned, the contrary takes place. He who trembles before God,... [he who] humbles himself, cries, shouts, sighs, and prays, it is he who wins; it is he who triumphs."[2]

PRAYER

Lord, keep me humble and praying, so that nothing divides us. Amen.

145
Divine Prototype

✠

From Psalm 145: "The LORD is gracious and merciful, slow to anger and abounding in steadfast love."[1]

In turn, how do I love our merciful God who never stops loving me?

ST. PIO'S WORDS

"All those who love Jesus must conform to this divine, eternal Model. . . . In His Humanity, Jesus desired to experience the incomprehensible suffering of being abandoned even by the heavenly Father. . . . Blessed are those souls who will be found in conformity with this divine Prototype, by having more greatly participated in His holy suffering. Therefore, humble yourself before God rather than become depressed in spirit. . . . Raise prayers of resignation and hope to Him, even when you fall due to weakness, and thank Him for the many graces with which He enriches you."[2]

"Live tranquilly, along with everyone else, and don't fear the storm caused by the evil one; he is powerless against souls in whom Jesus reigns."[3]

"When I consider the great goodness of the Lord . . . an irresistible impulse moves me to exclaim, 'Great is the Lord, and greatly to be praised!'[4]"[5]

PRAYER

Lord, You are great, indeed. I thank You for Your merciful love. Amen.

146
God, the "Fonder Mother"

✠

From Psalm 146: "Happy are those whose help is the God of Jacob, whose hope is in the LORD their God."[1]

Why would God take time to help miserable me?

ST. PIO'S WORDS

"Sacred Scripture assures you that an afflicted soul is united with its God: 'When they call to me, I will answer them; I will be with them in trouble, I will rescue them. . . .'[2] Take heart, then, and don't be afraid, for it is certain that the one who fears to be lost will not be lost, and the one who fights with eyes fixed on God will cry victory and intone the triumphal hymn. There is nothing to fear, for the heavenly Father has promised you the necessary help to prevent you from being overcome by temptations."[3]

"Don't give way to sadness, for the Lord is with you always. Aren't you in the hands of Providence, a fonder Mother than we can imagine? Take heart, then, for Jesus won't leave you for a single instant."[4]

"May His divine Majesty sustain you in your trouble and make you grow in His love."[5]

PRAYER

Lord, You are both Father and Mother to me, and I thank You. Amen.

147
When Fear and Love Unite

+

From Psalm 147: "The LORD takes pleasure in those who fear him."[1]

I don't understand how fearing God pleases Him.

ST. PIO'S WORDS

"When fear [of God] and love are united, they help each other, like brothers and sisters, to remain on their feet and walk securely in the Lord's paths. Love makes you hasten with rapid strides, while fear makes you watch prudently where you place your feet, and it guides you so that you may never stumble on the road leading to heaven."[2]

"You do well to desire to be united with Him every day, and the best proof of this is that, whenever you can, you never neglect to go to Jesus in the Blessed Sacrament to give and to receive His 'kiss' of peace.

"Calm yourself, then, and rejoice because in all this it is the Lord who is acting within you. You desire nothing else than to walk before Him all the time, so let Him guide you on the difficult journey of this life. Give Him your total assent so that He may act in the manner most pleasing to Him."[3]

PRAYER

Lord, I will fear and love You, now and forever. Thy will be done. Amen.

148
Because He Alone Is Worthy

✠

From Psalm 148: "Let them praise the name of the LORD, for his name alone is exalted; his glory is above earth and heaven."[1]

Sometimes it's hard to believe that His name, alone, is so important.

ST. PIO'S WORDS

"The climax of Christ's humiliation is found in His passion and death, when He submitted His human will to the will of His Father, endured great torments, and suffered the most-infamous death. . . . He humbled Himself, says St. Paul, and became obedient unto death, 'even death on a cross.'[2] As He was the only begotten Son of the Father, He was not induced to obey by fear of punishment. Neither did He obey for the sake of reward, as He Himself was God and equal in all things to the Father. His obedience, then — in view of His exalted position, and of the great difficulty of what was commanded, and of His willingness to comply with the heavenly Father's will — Jesus was highly pleasing to the eternal Father, who exalted Him and bestowed on Him 'the name that is above every name.'[3]

"It is by virtue of that name alone that you may hope to be saved.[4]"[5]

PRAYER

Lord Jesus Christ, I will praise Your name forever. Amen.

149
Song of Thanksgiving

✠

From Psalm 149: "Sing to the LORD a new song, his praise in the assembly of the faithful."[1]

Rather than always asking God for favors, I should praise Him.

ST. PIO'S WORDS

"Moved by gratitude and love, the blessed in heaven never cease to repeat [to God] what St. John the evangelist beheld in a vision: 'They sing a new song: You are worthy... for you were slaughtered and by your blood you ransomed for God saints from every tribe and language and people and nation.'[2]"[3]

"As I see the divine will being accomplished in you in everything, I truly cannot restrain myself from singing a hymn of thanksgiving to Jesus."[4]

"How I love your good soul because it doesn't want to love anything except our most-sweet Lord. How can a soul, who considers Jesus crucified for it, love anything but Him? And how can you shout like the angry people, 'Crucify Him!'[5]? Let Him be crucified in your heart.... Say, write, sing, and breathe: 'Long live Jesus!'"[6]

PRAYER

Lord, I will say, write, breathe, and sing Your praises forever. Amen.

150
Praise the Lord and Rejoice!

✠

From Psalm 150: "Let everything that breathes praise the LORD!"[1]

When darkness surrounds me, it's hard to praise God.

ST. PIO'S WORDS

"Rejoice at all times, for the Lord's yoke is an agreeable one. You are glorifying the Lord by your life, and He is pleased with you. Never leave any room in your heart for sadness, for this would be in conflict with the Holy Spirit poured into your soul."[2]

"'Blessed be God, the Father of our Lord Jesus Christ, the Father of mercies and God of all consolation. . . .'[3] May this good Father continue to show mercy and to console you in all the events of life. I really cannot tell you how grateful I am to so tender a Father for the many benefits He continues to lavish on you, in spite of your unworthiness and ingratitude. . . . May He be praised and blessed forever by all creatures."[4]

"Do not be frightened. . . . Rejoice, because when you least expect it, the Lord will make light shine in the darkness."[5]

"Rejoice, for Jesus is with you!"[6]

PRAYER

No matter what happens, You are with me. Praise You, Lord! Amen.

Source Notes

✠

$\mathcal{F}$or the sake of clarity, minor changes — including condensations and easier-to-understand terms — have been made to many of St. Padre Pio's quotes, all of which are taken from *Padre Pio of Pietrelcina's Letters, Volumes I, II,* and *III.* This list gives the location in *Padre Pio of Pietrelcina's Letters, Volumes I, II,* and *III,* where each quote used can be found, as well as the citations for quotes from *The Catholic Edition of the New Revised Standard Version Bible* (NRSV).

Introduction
1. *Volume I*, pages 753-754
2. Psalm 119:105, 114, 90
3. *Volume III*, page 895
4. Ibid., page 492
5. Ibid., page 310
6. Ibid., pages 102-103
7. Ibid., pages 728-729
8. John 14:1
9. *Volume III*, page 263
10. John 14:1
11. *Volume III*, page 491

Meditation 1
1. Psalm 1:1, 2, 3, 6
2. *Volume I*, page 730
3. *Volume II*, pages 469-70
4. Ibid., page 479

Meditation 2
1. Psalm 2:4, 11
2. 1 Corithians 10:13
3. *Volume II*, page 76

Meditation 3
1. Psalm 3: 1, 3
2. Genesis 15:1
3. *Volume III*, pages 177-178

Meditation 4
1. Psalm 4:3, 4
2. *Volume I*, page 1020

Meditation 5
1. Psalm 5:11
2. Philippians 2:10
3. Mark 16:17
4. Philippians 2:11
5. *Volume II*, pages 237-238

Meditation 6
1. Psalm 6:6, 8, 10
2. *Volume III*, page 1031

Meditation 7
1. Psalm 7:1, 2
2. 1 Peter 5:8, 9
3. *Volume II*, page 262

4. Ibid., page 187
5. *Volume III*, page 414
6. Ibid., page 423

Meditation 8
1. Psalm 8:3, 4, 5
2. *Volume III*, page 198
3. Ibid., page 800

Meditation 9
1. Psalm 9:9
2. *Volume II*, pages 488-489

Meditation 10
1. Psalm 10:1
2. Isaiah 58:10
3. *Volume III*, page 168
4. Ibid., page 78

Meditation 11
1. Psalm 11:5
2. *Volume II*, page 178
3. Galatians 2:20
4. See 2 Corinthians 12:9

Meditation 12
1. Psalm 12:1
2. *Volume II*, pages 358-359

Meditation 13
1. Psalm 13:1, 2
2. *Volume II*, pages 479-480

Meditation 14
1. Psalm 14:1
2. 1 Corinthians 10:13
3. Psalm 14:1
4. *Volume II*, pages 435-436

Meditation 15
1. Psalm 15:1, 2
2. *Volume III*, page 675
3. Ibid., page 674

4. Ibid., page 677

Meditation 16
1. Psalm 16:1, 2
2. *Volume III*, pages 279-280
3. Ibid., page 706

Meditation 17
1. Psalm 17:1
2. *Volume III*, page 873
3. Ibid., pages 747-748

Meditation 18
1. Psalm 18:1
2. *Volume II*, page 386
3. Ibid., page 423

Meditation 19
1. Psalm 19:9
2. *Volume I*, pages 456-457

Meditation 20
1. Psalm 20:1
2. Matthew 16:24
3 *Volume II*, pages 166-167

Meditation 21
1. Psalm 21:13
2. *Volume II*, page 87
3. *Volume III*, page 489
4. Ibid., page 564

Meditation 22
1. Psalm 22:1
2. Matthew 27:46
3. *Volume III*, page 873
4. Ibid., page 622
5. *Volume I*, page 1131

Meditation 23
1. Psalm 23:3
2. *Volume III*, page 249
3. Ibid., pages 262-263

4. Ibid., pages 297-298

Meditation 24
1. Psalm 24:6 and 5 (in that order)
2. *Volume III*, page 409
3. Ibid., pages 91-92

Meditation 25
1. Psalm 25:11
2. *Volume I*, pages 667-668

Meditation 26
1. Psalm 26:8
2. *Volume III*, pages 704-705
3. Ibid., page 553

Meditation 27
1. Psalm 27:1
2. 2 Corinthians 12:9
3. *Volume II*, pages 84-85
4. *Volume II*, page 86

Meditation 28
1. Psalm 28:9
2. *Volume III*, page 1040
3. *Volume II*, pages 231-232

Meditation 29
1. Psalm 29:11
2. Isaiah 38:17
3. *Volume III*, page 337
4. Ibid., page 308

Meditation 30
1. Psalm 30:5
2. *Volume III*, page 205
3. Ibid., page 492

Meditation 31
1. Psalm 31:5
2. *Volume III*, page 181
3. Galatians 2:20

4. Luke 23:46
5. *Volume III*, page 227

Meditation 32
1. Psalm 32:7
2. *Volume III*, page 324
3. *Volume II*, page 377

Meditation 33
1. Psalm 33:5
2. *Volume II*, page 508
3. *Volume II*, page 438
4. Song of Solomon 1:2
5. *Volume II*, page 508

Meditation 34
1. Psalm 34:7
2. *Volume II*, pages 420-421

Meditation 35
1. Psalm 35:22
2. *Volume II*, page 110
3. Ibid., page 111
4. Ibid., page 240

Meditation 36
1. Psalm 36:7
2. *Volume II*, pages 152-153

Meditation 37
1. Psalm 37:7
2. *Volume II*, page 189
3. Ibid., pages 189-190
4. Proverbs 10:19
5. *Volume III*, page 436
6. Ibid., page 363

Meditation 38
1. Psalm 38:9
2. *Volume II*, pages 422-423

Meditation 39
1. Psalm 39:4

2. Philippians 1:20-21
3. *Volume II*, page 356

Meditation 40
1. Psalm 40:8
2. Matthew 6:10
3. Ibid., 6:11
4. Ibid., 6:10
5. *Volume II*, pages 358-359

Meditation 41
1. Psalm 41:5, 7
2. *Volume II*, page 410
3. Ibid., pages 410-411

Meditation 42
1. Psalm 42:1, 2
2. *Volume II*, page 542

Meditation 43
1. Psalm 43:3
2. *Volume III*, page 404
3. Ibid., page 175

Meditation 44
1. Psalm 44:23
2. Matthew 14:30, 31
3. *Volume III*, page 936

Meditation 45
1. Psalm 45:9
2. Luke 1:38
3. Ibid., 1:46, 47, 48
4. *Volume II*, page 436
5. Ibid., page 389

Meditation 46
1. Psalm 46:10
2. *Volume III*, pages 990-991
3. Ibid., page 769

Meditation 47
1. Psalm 47:2

2. Luke 1:46, 47
3. *Volume III*, page 101

Meditation 48
1. Psalm 48:14
2. *Volume III*, page 541
3. *Volume II*, page 534
4. *Volume III*, page 540
5. Ibid., page 352

Meditation 49
1. Psalm 49:17
2. Colossians 3:2
3. *Volume II*, page 243

Meditation 50
1. Psalm 50:14
2. *Volume II*, page 316
3. Ibid., page 366
4. Ibid., page 384

Meditation 51
1. Psalm 51:11
2. *Volume III*, page 305
3. Ibid., page 255

Meditation 52
1. Psalm 52:8
2. Proverbs 23:26
3. Matthew 25:1-13
4. *Volume II*, page 489

Meditation 53
1. Psalm 53:5
2. *Volume III*, pages 72-73

Meditation 54
1. Psalm 54:1
2. *Volume III*, page 582
3. Ibid., page 583

Meditation 55
1. Psalm 55:2

2. *Volume II*, page 169
3. Ibid., page 66

Meditation 56
1. Psalm 56:8
2. *Volume II*, page 89
3. Ibid., page 353

Meditation 57
1. Psalm 57:1
2. *Volume III*, page 115
3. Ibid., page 150
4. *Volume II*, page 84
5. *Volume III*, page 104

Meditation 58
1. Psalm 58:1-2
2. *Volume III*, pages 58-59
3. Ibid., page 58

Meditation 59
1. Psalm 59:16
2. Psalm 42:1
3. *Volume III*, pages 107-108

Meditation 60
1. Psalm 60:10
2. Romans 4:25
3. *Volume II*, pages 212-213

Meditation 61
1. Psalm 61:2
2. 2 Corinthians 12:9
3. 1 Corinthians 10:13
4. *Volume III*, page 250

Meditation 62
1. Psalm 62:10
2. *Volume III*, page 250
3. Ibid., page 320
4. Ibid., page 369
5. Ibid., page 281

Meditation 63
1. Psalm 63:1
2. *Volume II*, page 141

Meditation 64
1. Psalm 64:8
2. *Volume II*, pages 246-247
3. Ibid., page 249
4. Ibid., page 549

Meditation 65
1. Psalm 65:4
2. *Volume III*, page 249
3. Romans 8:29
4. *Volume III*, page 200

Meditation 66
1. Psalm 66:3
2. *Volume III*, page 355
3. Ibid., page 179

Meditation 67
1. Psalm 67:4
2. *Volume III*, page 779
3. Matthew 5:16
4. *Volume III*, pages 778-779

Meditation 68
1. Psalm 68:20
2. *Volume III*, pages 252-253
3. Ibid., page 580

Meditation 69
1. Psalm 69:2
2. Luke 7:48
3. Psalm 69:2
4. Psalm 69:15
5. *Volume III*, pages 218-219

Meditation 70
1. Psalm 70:5
2. Hebrews 4:15

3. Colossians 1:24
4. *Volume III*, pages 353-354

Meditation 71
1. Psalm 71:9
2. *Volume III*, page 532
3. Ibid., page 267

Meditation 72
1. Psalm 72:7
2. *Volume III*, page 333

Meditation 73
1. Psalm 73:28
2. *Volume III*, page 89
3. Ibid., page 90
4. Ibid., page 452

Meditation 74
1. Psalm 74:17
2. *Volume III*, page 321

Meditation 75
1. Psalm 75:4, 7
2. *Volume III*, pages 341-342
3. Ibid., page 297
4. Ibid., page 350

Meditation 76
1. Psalm 76:8, 9
2. *Volume III*, pages 343-344

Meditation 77
1. Psalm 77:8
2. 1Corinthians 10:13
3. *Volume II*, pages 68-69
4. Hebrews 4:15
5. Matthew 27:46
6. *Volume II*, page 68

Meditation 78
1. Psalm 78:24, 25
2. *Volume I*, page 426

3. Matthew 6:11
4. *Volume II*, page 357

Meditation 79
1. Psalm 79:5
2. *Volume III*, pages 318-319

Meditation 80
1. Psalm 80:7
2. *Volume II*, pages 122-123

Meditation 81
1. Psalm 81:16
2. *Volume III*, pages 288-289

Meditation 82
1. Psalm 82:4
2. *Volume II*, page 139

Meditation 83
1. Psalm 83:2
2. *Volume II*, pages 76-77

Meditation 84
1. Psalm 84:10
2. Ibid.
3. *Volume III*, page 572

Meditation 85
1. Psalm 85:10
2. *Volume III*, page 327
3. Psalm 85:10
4. *Volume II*, pages 425-426
5. Ibid., page 508

Meditation 86
1. Psalm 86:11
2. Matthew 6:10
3. *Volume III*, page 57

Meditation 87
1. Psalm 87:3
2. 2 Corinthians 12:2-4

3. Galatians 2:20
4. *Volume III*, pages 283-284
5. Ibid., page 713

Meditation 88
1. Psalm 88:3
2. Sirach 2:4, 5
3. *Volume II*, pages 167-168

Meditation 89
1. Psalm 89:41, 42
2. Luke 14:11
3. Colossians 2:9
4. *Volume II*, page 236

Meditation 90
1. Psalm 90:15
2. Ibid.
3. 2 Corinthians 4:17
4. *Volume II*, page 168

Meditation 91
1. Psalm 91:11, 12
2. *Volume III*, pages 84-85
3. *Volume II*, page 478

Meditation 92
1. Psalm 92:1
2. Matthew 4
3. *Volume III*, page 94
4. Ibid., page 107
5. Ibid., page 410

Meditation 93
1. Psalm 93:1
2. *Volume III*, pages 312-313
3. Ibid., pages 207-208
4. Ibid., page 297

Meditation 94
1. Psalm 94:14
2. *Volume III*, page 1018

3. Ibid., page 1017

Meditation 95
1. Psalm 95:2
2. *Volume II*, page 290
3. Ibid., page 291

Meditation 96
1. Psalm 96:13
2. *Volume II*, page 69
3. *Volume III*, page 248

Meditation 97
1. Psalm 97:10
2. *Volume I*, page 223
3. *Volume III*, page 365

Meditation 98
1. Psalm 98:4
2. John 16:22
3. *Volume II*, page 214

Meditation 99
1. Psalm 99:3
2. *Volume II*, page 110
3. Ibid., page 274
4. Ibid., page 70
5. Ibid., page 274

Meditation 100
1. Psalm 100:3
2. *Volume III*, page 307

Meditation 101
1. Psalm 101:7
2. *Volume III*, pages 213-214
3. Ibid., page 360
4. Philippians 4:13

Meditation 102
1. Psalm 102:7
2. *Volume III*, page 85
3. *Volume II*, page 292

4. Ibid., page 421
5. Ibid., page 420

Meditation 103
1. Psalm 103:10
2. Esther 8:3, 8
3. *Volume II*, page 504
4. Ibid., page 506

Meditation 104
1. Psalm 104:1, 2
2. *Volume II*, page 86
3. Psalm 91:15
4. *Volume II*, page 320

Meditation 105
1. Psalm 105: 8, 9
2. James 4:6
3. Mark 14:38
4. *Volume II*, pages 500-501
5. Ibid., page 505

Meditation 106
1. Psalm 106:48
2. Luke 21:19
3. *Volume I*, pages 992-993

Meditation 107
1. Psalm 107:28
2. Ibid., 91:15
3. James 1:2
4. *Volume I*, pages 1128-1129

Meditation 108
1. Psalm 108:13
2. *Volume I*, pages 644-645

Meditation 109
1. Psalm 109:22
2. *Volume III*, pages 608-609

Meditation 110
1. Psalm 110:1

2. 1 Peter 5:8
3. *Volume II*, pages 262-263

Meditation 111
1. Psalm 111:10
2. *Volume III*, page 276

Meditation 112
1. Psalm 112:10
2. Luke 21:18
3. *Volume II*, pages 448-449

Meditation 113
1. Psalm 113:5, 6
2. *Volume II*, page 260
3. Sirach 2:10
4. *Volume II*, page 260

Meditation 114
1. Psalm 114:7
2. *Volume III*, pages 719-720

Meditation 115
1. Psalm 115:11
2. Romans 8:28
3. *Volume III*, pages 730-731

Meditation 116
1. Psalm 116:1
2. *Volume III*, pages 830-831

Meditation 117
1. Psalm 117:2
2. *Volume II*, pages 542-543

Meditation 118
1. Psalm 118:22
2. *Volume III*, pages 64-65

Meditation 119
1. Psalm 119:32
2. Ibid.
3. Luke 21:19

4. *Volume I*, pages 1105-1106

Meditation 120
1. Psalm 120:6
2. *Volume I*, page 674
3. Ibid., page 678

Meditation 121
1. Psalm 121:7
2. *Volume I*, page 1029

Meditation 122
1. Psalm 122:1
2. *Volume III*, pages 88-90

Meditation 123
1. Psalm 123:2
2. *Volume III*, pages 60-61

Meditation 124
1. Psalm 124:1, 5
2. *Volume I*, pages 690-691

Meditation 125
1. Psalm 125:2
2. *Volume III*, pages 25-26

Meditation 126
1. Psalm 126:3
2. *Volume I*, page 308

Meditation 127
1. Psalm 127:1
2. *Volume III*, pages 702-703

Meditation 128
1. Psalm 128:2
2. *Volume I*, pages 1022-1023

Meditation 129
1. Psalm 129:2
2. Luke 21:18
3. *Volume I*, pages 665-666

Meditation 130
1. Psalm 130:1
2. *Volume II*, page 387

Meditation 131
1. Psalm 131:1, 2
2. Matthew 18:3
3. *Volume I*, pages 677-678

Meditation 132
1. Psalm 132:13, 14
2. Galatians 2:20
3. *Volume I*, page 431
4. *Volume III*, page 51
5. Ibid., page 50

Meditation 133
1. Psalm 133:3
2. John 17:24
3. *Volume II*, pages 211-212

Meditation 134
1. Psalm 134:2
2. Ibid.
3. *Volume III*, page 634

Meditation 135
1. Psalm 135:5, 6
2. Psalm 118:23
3. Ibid.
4. *Volume I*, pages 889-890

Meditation 136
1. Psalm 136:1
2. *Volume I*, page 644
3. Ibid., page 645
4. Psalm 136:1
5. *Volume II*, page 431

Meditation 137
1. Psalm 137:4
2. *Volume I*, page 725

Meditation 138
1. Psalm 138:8
2. *Volume I*, page 357

Meditation 139
1. Psalm 139:10
2. *Volume III*, pages 714-715

Meditation 140
1. Psalm 140:1, 2
2. *Volume I*, pages 244-245
3. Ibid., page 254
4. Ibid., page 245

Meditation 141
1. Psalm 141:3
2. *Volume III*, pages 90-91
3. Ibid., page 357

Meditation 142
1. Psalm 142:3, 6
2. Psalm 103:13
3. *Volume I*, pages 346-347

Meditation 143
1. Psalm 143:10
2. Galatians 5:25
3. *Volume II*, pages 216-218
4. Ibid., page 420

Meditation 144
1. Psalm 144:7
2. *Volume III*, page 98

Meditation 145
1. Psalm 145:8
2. *Volume III*, page 611
3. Ibid., page 606
4. Psalm 145:3
5. *Volume I*, page 781

Meditation 146
1. Psalm 146:5
2. Psalm 91:15
3. *Volume II*, page 411
4. Ibid., page 253
5. Ibid., page 254

Meditation 147
1. Psalm 147:11
2. *Volume II*, page 85
3. Ibid., page 87

Meditation 148
1. Psalm 148:13
2. Philippians 2:8
3. Ibid., 2:9
4. Acts 4:12
5. *Volume II*, page 237

Meditation 149
1. Psalm 149:1
2. Revelation 5:9
3. *Volume II*, page 237
4. *Volume III*, page 57
5. Mark 15:13
6. *Volume III*, page 332

Meditation 150
1. Psalm 150:6
2. *Volume II*, page 251
3. 2 Corinthians 1:3
4. *Volume II*, page 277
5. Ibid., page 307
6. Ibid., page 303

Bibliography

✠

Di Flumeri, Father Gerardo, O.F.M. Cap. *Homage To Padre Pio*. San Giovanni Rotondo, Italy: Our Lady of Grace Capuchin Friary, 1982.

Di Flumeri, Father Gerardo, O.F.M. Cap., editor. *Padre Pio of Pietrelcina Letters, Volumes I and II*. San Giovanni Rotondo: Italy, 1994.

Gaudiose, Dorothy M. *Prophet of the People*. New York: Alba House, 1974.

McGregor, Fr. Augustine, O.C.S.O. *Padre Pio: His Early Years*. San Giovanni Rotondo, Italy: Our Lady of Grace Capuchin Friary, 1981.

The New Revised Standard Version Bible: Catholic Edition. Nashville, Tennessee: Catholic Bible Press, 1993.

Parente, Father Alessio, O.F.M. Cap., editor. *Padre Pio of Pietrelcina Letters, Volume III*. San Giovanni Rotondo: Italy.

Parente, Fr. Alessio, O.F.M. Cap. *Send Me your Guardian Angel*. San Giovanni Rotondo, Italy: Our Lady of Grace Capuchin Friary, 1984.

Ruffin, C. Bernard. *Padre Pio: The True Story (Revised and Expanded)*. Huntington, Indiana: Our Sunday Visitor, Inc., 1991.

Schug, Rev. John A., Cap. *Padre Pio: He Bore the Stigmata*. Huntington, Indiana: Our Sunday Visitor, Inc., 1976.

United States Catholic Conference, *Catechism of the Catholic Church, Second Edition*. United States Catholic Conference, Inc. — Libreria Editrice Vaticana, 1997.

Resources

✠

Resources who provide information on St. Padre Pio for the author and for all who are interested in learning more about Pio:

National Centre for Padre Pio, Inc.
The Vera M. Calandra Family
2213 Old Route 100
Barto, PA 19504
Telephone: (610) 845-3000
Fax: (610) 845-2666
E-mail: ncfpp@earthlink.net
Website: www.ncfpp.com

Our Lady of Grace Capuchin Friary
71013 San Giovanni Rotondo
Foggia, Italy
Telephone: (0882) 418305
Fax: (0882) 418327
E-mail: postulazione@vocedipadrepio.com
Website: www. vocedipadrepio.com

Index

＋

About the Author

✠

Since 1989, Eileen Dunn Bertanzetti has worked as an instructor for The Institute of Children's Literature. During that time, she has sold more than 175 articles and stories to markets such as *Our Sunday Visitor* newspaper, *Catholic Heritage*, *The Family Digest*, *St. Anne de Beaupre* (Canada), Association of Marian Helpers, *Queen of Hearts*, The Institute of Children's Literature website, *Children's Writer*, *Classroom Computer Learning*, and Christian Education Publishers. In 1999, Our Sunday Visitor published Eileen's book of meditations for adults, *Padre Pio's Words of Hope*. In 2002, Pauline Books and Media published Eileen's *Saint Pio of Pietrelcina: Rich In Love*, a biography for young adults. Also in 2002, Chelsea House Publishers published Eileen's biography for children, *Molly Pitcher: Heroine*. In March of 2004, Our Sunday Visitor published Eileen's book *Praying In the Presence of Our Lord with St. Padre Pio*.

An Elementary Education graduate of Lock Haven University of Pennsylvania, Eileen stays in touch with the needs and interests of readers through her extended family and friends; through her involvement in her local parish as Eucharistic Minister and Lector; through her volunteer work at the local nursing home; and through her work with The Institute of Children's Literature.

Summary of Eileen's Publishing Credits

A. Books (in chronological order):

1. *Padre Pio's Words of Hope*, meditations, adults, Our Sunday Visitor, 1999

2. *Saint Pio of Pietrelcina: Rich In Love*, biography, eleven-year-olds through young adults, Pauline Books & Media, 2002

3. *Molly Pitcher: Heroine*, biography, 2nd- through 6th-graders, Chelsea House Publishers, 2002

4. *Praying In the Presence of Our Lord with St. Padre Pio*, meditations, adults, Our Sunday Visitor, 2004

5. *Poor Pio*, biography, young children, Hard Shell Word Factory, 2006

B. Eileen sold more than 175 articles and stories to the following publishers:

1. *Catholic Heritage*
2. Christian Education Publishers
3. *Children's Writer*
4. *Parish Family Digest*
5. *Finnish Signs of the Times* (in Finland)
6. *Queen of All Hearts*
7. *St. Ann de Beaupre* (Canadian magazine)
8. *Christian Living*
9. Association of Marian Helpers' *Thirteenth of the Month Club*
10. *Primary Treasure*
11. *Discovery Trails*
12. *My Friend*
13. *R-A-D-A-R*
14. *Between Times*
15. *Classroom Computer Learning*
16. *On the Line*
17. *Alive! For Young Teens*
18. *Computer Learning Month*
19. Barrington House Publishing
20. *The Music Leader*
21. *Our Little Friend*

Newspapers:

22. *Our Sunday Visitor*
23. *The Catholic Register*
24. *Lock Haven Express*
25. *Clinton Times*

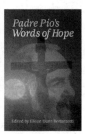